# 350 Years of New Castle, Delaware

*Chapters in a Town's History*

*Detail from aerial view of New Castle, ca. early 1960s.
(Courtesy of the Historical Society of Delaware.)*

*350 Years of*
# New Castle, Delaware
*Chapters in a Town's History*

CONSTANCE J. COOPER, EDITOR

Published in Honor of the 350th Anniversary
of the Founding of New Castle, Delaware

New Castle Historical Society
New Castle, Delaware
Cedar Tree Books
Wilmington, Delaware
2001

First Edition

Published by **Cedar Tree Books**
Nine Germay Drive, Wilmington, DE 19804
and **The New Castle Historical Society**
2 East Fourth Street, New Castle, DE 19720

ISBN: 1–892142–12–0

Title: 350 Years of New Castle, Delaware
Editor: Constance J. Cooper
Book Design: Angela Werner, Michael Höhne Design

Copyright:© 2001 New Castle Historical Society

**Library of Congress Cataloging-in-Publication Data**

350 Years of New Castle, Delaware: chapters in a town's history / edited
   by Constance J. Cooper
      p. cm.
   "Published in Honor of the 350th Anniversary of the Founding of New
   Castle, Delaware."
   ISBN 1-892142-12-0
   1. New Castle (Del.)--History. I. Title: Three hundred fifty years of New
   Castle, Delaware. II. Cooper, Constance J.

F174.N5 A15 2001
975.1'1--dc21

2001042222

ALL RIGHTS RESERVED:
No part of this book may be reproduced in any manner without the
express written consent of the publisher, except in the case of brief excerpts in
critical reviews and articles.

Printed in the United States of America on 60# archival, acid-free paper meeting
the requirements of the American Standard for Permanence of Paper for printed
Library Materials.

# Table of Contents

Preface . . . . . . . . . . . . . . . . . . . . . . . . . . . . . . . . . . . . . . vii
Publisher's Foreword . . . . . . . . . . . . . . . . . . . . . . . . . . . . viii
Foreword . . . . . . . . . . . . . . . . . . . . . . . . . . . . . . . . . . . . . . ix
Acknowledgments . . . . . . . . . . . . . . . . . . . . . . . . . . . . . . xi
Contributors . . . . . . . . . . . . . . . . . . . . . . . . . . . . . . . . . . xiii
Introduction . . . . . . . . . . . . . . . . . . . . . . . . . . . . . . . . . . xv

Chapter One: The City of Amsterdam's Colony on the
    Delaware, 1656–1664, *C.A. Weslager* . . . . . . . . . . . . . . . . . . 1

Voices and Viewpoints: *The Reverend George Ross* . . . . . . . . 31

Chapter Two: Great Expectations, Practical
    Accomplishments: New Castle, 1700–1750,
    *William R. Cario* . . . . . . . . . . . . . . . . . . . . . . . . . . . . . . . 35

Voices and Viewpoints: *Early Travelers' Impressions* . . . . . . . 69

Chapter Three: A Town Among Cities: New Castle,
    1780–1840, *Constance J. Cooper* . . . . . . . . . . . . . . . . . . . . . 73

Voices and Viewpoints: *Fire! 1824* . . . . . . . . . . . . . . . . . . . 109

Chapter Four: Manufactural Interests and Industries,
    *Alexander B. Cooper* . . . . . . . . . . . . . . . . . . . . . . . . . . . . 113

Voices and Viewpoints: *African Americans* . . . . . . . . . . . . . 129

Chapter Five: New Castle Memories, 1900–1950 . . . . . . . 135

Voices and Viewpoints: *Preserving a Treasure Town* . . . . . . 151

Chapter Six: "The Gospel of New Castle": Historic
    Preservation in a Delaware Town,
    *Deborah Van Riper Harper* . . . . . . . . . . . . . . . . . . . . . . . 155

Selected New Castle Bibliography Through 2001,
    *Stephen J. Cordano* . . . . . . . . . . . . . . . . . . . . . . . . . . . . 189

# Preface

This commemorative volume was conceived as an historic tribute to the three hundred and fifty years that have passed since the founding of New Castle on the Delaware in 1651. The desire to hold a special celebration was inspired by the Tercentenary held in 1951, recalling the Dutch roots of the town's inception. Following a public meeting called by the Mayor of New Castle in the summer of 2000, the resulting Steering Committee and its chairpersons set about to honor all the varied participants who have played a part in making New Castle the special national wonder that we who live here call our home. It is hoped that the reader will delight in this book and take pride in knowing that such an American treasure is still being lovingly preserved.

*Robert C. Sigmund*
*Civic and Cultural Commissioner*
*for the 350th Anniversary Celebration*

## Publisher's Foreword

When Cedar Tree Press began its historical book series in 1990, the volumes were intended solely for free distribution to our customers during the holiday season. After a few years, because of the historical significance of these works, we decided that they merited wider dissemination and began reprinting earlier editions and increasing the quantity of our printings.

This is our first collaboration in publishing a volume in the series, and what a wonderful topic to collaborate on. The history of New Castle, founded well before the birth of our nation, needs to be chronicled not only for us but for the generations that we are responsible for, and who will remember us for affording them a view of the past.

*Nicholas L. Cerchio III*
*Publisher*

# Foreword

The New Castle Historical Society is very pleased to co-sponsor the publication of *350 Years of New Castle, Delaware: Chapters in a Town's History* in connection with the 350th anniversary celebration of the founding of Delaware's most historic town. One of the Society's main purposes is to promote, in all appropriate ways, the publication and compilation of materials relating to New Castle's history. The Society believes that the publication of this work is a splendid contribution to the appreciation and preservation of historical information about New Castle, and the Society is honored to have assisted in its publication.

The New Castle Historical Society, founded in 1934, operates the Amstel House, the Dutch House, and the Old Library Museum. It regularly sponsors exhibits and programs on varied topics of historical interest. The most recent exhibit of the Society, recognizing contributions of African Americans to New Castle history over the centuries, will open in October 2001 to coincide with the many other 350th anniversary festivities. This newest exhibit underscores the Society's commitment to interpret all facets of New Castle's history—including areas that may not have been sufficiently emphasized previously—in order to add to a deeper and broader understanding of all components of New Castle's fascinating history. The Society extends its best wishes for a successful 350th anniversary celebration.

*Richard Rodney Cooch*
*President, New Castle Historical Society*

## Acknowledgments

Many individuals and institutions helped make the creation of this book both possible and pleasurable. Robert C. Sigmund, Civic and Cultural Commissioner for the New Castle 350th Celebration, Stephen J. Cordano, chair of the Publications Committee, and Robert Fleck of Oak Knoll Press conceived the idea of a commemorative volume and supported it every step of the way. The New Castle Historical Society, Richard R. Cooch, President, and Ms. Bruce Dalleo, Executive Director, and Cedar Tree Books, Nicholas L. Cerchio III, President, graciously agreed to publish this tribute to one of Delaware's oldest communities. John von Hoelle, Publishing Director of Oak Knoll Press, provided valuable assistance with design and production.

Special thanks go to William R. Cario, Stephen J. Cordano, and Deborah Van Riper Harper for their contributions to the book. The writings of Alexander B. Cooper and C.A. Weslager are used posthumously, with appreciation.

Several libraries and individuals have kindly allowed the publication of materials from their collections:

**Delaware Public Archives, Dover:** image of Immanuel Church
**Robert Montgomery Bird and The Winterthur Library:**
   **Decorative Arts Photographic Collection:** watercolors by Robert Montgomery Bird of Tile House and Town Hall and Market House.
**Special Collections, Morris Library, University of Delaware:** quotation from letter of the Rev. George Ross, March 27, 1750

**New Castle Historical Society:**
"New Castle Today" from *New Castle on the Delaware* (New Castle Historical Society, 1936), pp. 19–21
Illustrations from Horace Deakyne Collection as indicated in credit lines

**Historical Society of Delaware,** Wilmington:
Deborah Van Riper Harper, "'The Gospel of New Castle': Historic Preservation in a Delaware Town," reprinted from *Delaware History* 25 (1992–93): 77–105
C.A. Weslager, introduction to "The City of Amsterdam's Colony on the Delaware, 1656–1664; With Unpublished Dutch Notarial Abstracts," reprinted from *Delaware History* 20 (1982–83): 2–19
Alexander B. Cooper, "Manufactural Interests and Industries," Section 41, and paragraph on Peter Jackson from Section 40, page 4, from "The History of New Castle, Delaware, From Its First Settlement to the Present Time, 1651–1907"
Maria Booth Rogers to James Rogers, [April 27, 1824], Boothhurst Collection
George Harrison to George Read II, April 19, 1803, Richard S. Rodney Collection
Brochure, "New Castle Delaware: A Report Concerning Its History and Future," 1949, New Castle Restoration Papers
Dust jacket illustration, *New Castle Waterfront* by Robert Shaw
Illustrations as indicated in credit lines

Finally, the editor would like to thank her friends and colleagues at the Historical Society of Delaware for their assistance and support.

## Contributors

WILLIAM R. CARIO is Associate Professor of History and Assistant Vice President of Academics at Concordia University Wisconsin in Mequon, Wisconsin. He earned his Ph.D. at New York University. This article is drawn from his dissertation, "Anglicization in a 'Frenchified, Scotchified, Dutchified Place': New Castle, Delaware, 1690–1750."

ALEXANDER B. COOPER (1844–1924) was a lawyer in New Castle and an avocational historian. His articles on New Castle were published in the *Wilmington Sunday Star* in 1907 and 1908.

CONSTANCE J. COOPER is Manuscript Librarian and Managing Editor at the Historical Society of Delaware in Wilmington. She received her Ph.D. from the University of Delaware. Her article is drawn from her dissertation, "A Town Among Cities: New Castle, Delaware, 1780–1840."

STEPHEN J. CORDANO, a New Castle resident and avocational historian, is chair of the Publications Committee for the New Castle 350th Celebration. He received his MBA degree from the University of Southern California.

DEBORAH VAN RIPER HARPER received her M.A. in history from the University of Delaware and is Associate Curator of Education at the Winterthur Museum, Winterthur, Delaware.

C.A. WESLAGER (1909–1994) of Wilmington wrote over 100 books and articles on Delaware history and archaeology. He specialized in American Indians and Delaware's early Dutch and Swedish settlements.

# Introduction

In its 350 years, New Castle, Delaware, has had many identities. Founded in 1651 as Fort Casimir, a Dutch response to the Swedes' Fort Christina a few miles north, near modern Wilmington, the new settlement underwent several changes of ownership and name during its first generation alone. Fort Casimir and the spit of land on which it stood disappeared long ago, but the village surrounding it grew into the city of New Castle.

Colonial New Castle served as the seat of New Castle County, the capital of the three counties that became the state of Delaware, and as a port. Many eighteenth-century immigrants, especially Scots-Irish, entered the colonies at New Castle. Being the oldest town on this part of the Delaware River did not automatically make New Castle the most successful, however. Philadelphia, founded in 1681, and then Wilmington some fifty years later, provided stiff competition. New Castle quickly learned that those places would affect and limit its growth.

In the early days of the new nation, New Castle found a niche as a transportation hub, a vital link in the journey via land and water from Philadelphia to Baltimore. Development of this asset led to the construction of the New Castle and Frenchtown Railroad, one of the nation's earliest railroads. Yet even this advantage lasted only briefly, for a few years later the Philadelphia, Wilmington and Baltimore Railroad offered more convenient, direct rail transportation between those cities. New Castle's political role changed, too. In 1777,

Delaware's capital moved to Dover. Threats to move the county seat to Wilmington punctuated the nineteenth century and finally succeeded in 1881.

From the 1830s on, industry shaped New Castle's life. The town pioneered the manufacture of railroad engines, first by the New Castle and Frenchtown Railroad and then by the New Castle Manufacturing Company. Other firms came and went through the first half of the twentieth century, producing a variety of goods.

Once it lost its roles as a transportation and political center, New Castle became a quiet town. For the most part people did not remodel their homes to keep up with current styles or tear down and replace older structures. Some newer buildings were erected, of course, but they fit in comfortably with existing ones. Yet this very lack of dramatic change created the built environment that shapes New Castle's current identity as an architectural and historical treasure town.

In honor of New Castle's 350 years, this book presents articles, primary sources, and illustrations that tell many parts of New Castle's story. But even though the contents range from the 1650s to 1950, the book does not claim to be a complete history of the town. Many wonderful stories and pictures had to be left out for lack of space, and many aspects of New Castle's history have yet to be studied. Consider this volume an introduction, and an invitation, to the history of one of Delaware's oldest, most significant, and most beautiful towns.

# Chapter One

This article, adapted from a longer piece, tells of New Castle during some of its earliest years, when it was owned by the City of Amsterdam and called New Amstel. The article originally appeared as the introduction to "The City of Amsterdam's Colony on the Delaware, 1656–1664; with Unpublished Dutch Notarial Abtracts" in *Delaware History* 20 (1982–83): 1–26, 73–97 and is reprinted with permission.

# The City of Amsterdam's Colony on the Delaware, 1656–1664

## C. A. Weslager

An agreement became official on August 16, 1656, whereby the City of Amsterdam consented to plant a colony in the New Netherland on lands formerly under the control of the Dutch West India Company.[1] After subsequent discussion, the burgomasters of the City decided on November 4, 1656, to assume jurisdiction over Fort Casimir and the houses clustered around it (present New Castle, Delaware).[2] Seven years later, December 22, 1663, the Company transferred to the City the entire Delaware (or South) River region, "from the sea upwards to as far as the river reaches, on the east-side inland three leagues from the bank of the river, on the west-side as far as the territory reaches to the English colony [Maryland]...."[3]

All the land comprising the present state of Delaware was included in the latter transaction. This is the only instance the writer has found—a situation which has no parallel in American colonial history—whereby a European city took over the ownership and governance of a colony. To bring this transaction into proper perspective, it is necessary to review briefly certain events which are fully discussed in the historical literature.[4]

The City's acquisition had been preceded by three decades of international rivalry and dispute over the control of the Delaware River valley. One of the principal contenders was the Dutch West India Company, chartered in the Netherlands on June 3, 1621, with exclusive rights to trade in specified foreign waters, including the full sweep of the North and South American coasts. The government also gave the Company power to negotiate treaties with the Indians, establish and govern colonies, administer justice, fly its own flag, and appoint governors and other civil and military officials.[5] Thus, Dutch exploration and settlement of the New Netherland was not undertaken by the government but was sponsored by a commercial organization with the express purpose of earning dividends for its investors. It is customary to think of New York State as constituting the New Netherland, but Delaware, New Jersey, and parts of Pennsylvania and Connecticut were also included.

The first Dutch settlement within the bounds of present Delaware was made at Swanendael (present Lewes) in 1631 by patroons who were associated with the Dutch West India Company The original colony consisted of twenty-eight men, later increased to thirty-two.[6] The men were expected to fish for whales and obtain whale oil and also to raise tobacco and grains, all of which were in demand in Holland. If the venture succeeded, the patroons intended to send women and children and expand the colony, but within a year the Indians destroyed the buildings and killed all the men.[7]

Despite the failure of the patroons' colony at Swanendael, the West India Company conducted a lucrative fur-trading business with the Indians. Initially the company had a virtual monopoly on the Delaware River and its tributaries in this profitable enterprise, but

## Chapter 1 – The City of Amsterdam's Colony

the English and Swedes soon provided competition. In 1638, the Swedes built a fort at what is now Wilmington, naming both it and the river on which it stood after Christina, the child queen of Sweden. The English attempted to make a settlement on the Schuylkill River and another on the Salem River in New Jersey as they tried to establish trading relations with the Indians.[8] Lord Baltimore also settled a proprietary colony in Maryland south of the New Netherland, and he claimed ownership of what is now Delaware according to the terms of his charter from the king of England.[9]

Petrus Stuyvesant was commissioned director-general of the New Netherland by the directors of the West India Company in 1647, with his headquarters at New Amsterdam on Manhattan Island (present New York City). Animal pelts obtained from the Indians by Dutch traders on the Delaware and elsewhere were accumulated here and shipped to Holland, where men's hats were made from beaver

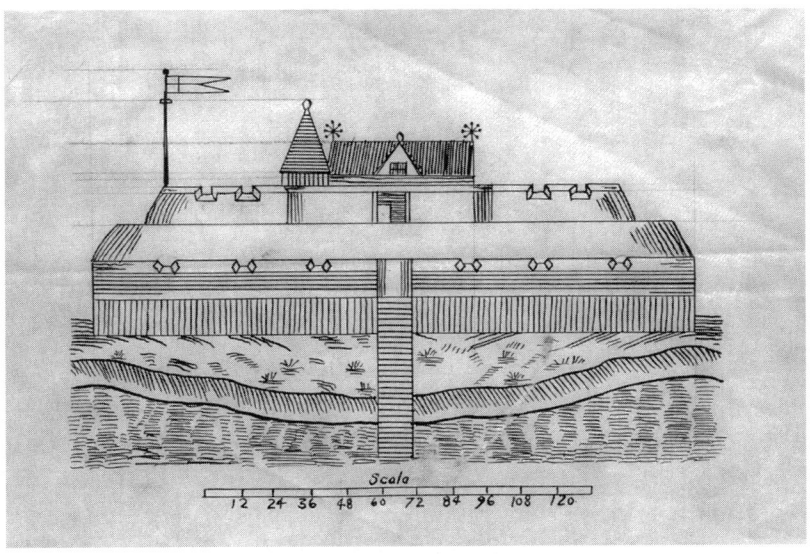

*Fort Casimir, late 1800s–early 1900s, redrawn from sketch in Peter Lindestrom's* Geographia Americae *(1655).*
*(Courtesy of the Historical Society of Delaware.)*

skins and coats, robes, gloves, and other apparel were fashioned from animal skins. As the Swedish colony on the Delaware grew, competition for the fur trade became more heated, and the Swedes undersold the Dutch and took business away from them. Stuyvesant felt compelled to take military action to protect the Company's interests.

In 1651, Stuyvesant marched overland from Manhattan with a force of about 125 soldiers, rendezvousing with a fleet of Dutch vessels that had sailed down the coast into Delaware Bay and up the river to join him. The Swedes were not strong enough to repel this invasion, and the Swedish governor, Johan Printz, offered no resistance. Stuyvesant paid off the Indians to extinguish their rights to the land, and built Fort Casimir on a site that dominated the river. Leaving a small garrison at the new fort to secure Dutch sovereignty, he returned to Manhattan with his forces.[10]

As time passed, Fort Casimir began to deteriorate as a result of inattention, and Stuyvesant lacked sufficient funds to repair it and reinforce the garrison. In 1654, a new Swedish governor, Johan Rising, arrived with supplies and additional settlers. He seized the fort, rebuilt it, and renamed it Fort Trinity.

For the second time, Stuyvesant was forced to retaliate, and the Company made men, ships, and materiel available to him. In August of 1655, he again invaded New Sweden with a strong fleet and a military force greatly outnumbering the Swedish defenders. Among the vessels in his flotilla was *de Wagh*, a man-of-war belonging to the City of Amsterdam, which the Company had chartered for the expedition. The Dutch soldiers killed cattle, goats, swine, and poultry, and plundered the Swedish and Finnish farms. They recaptured Fort Trinity, and Stuyvesant restored the name that he had given it, Fort Casimir. Fort Christina was seized and renamed Fort Altena. Governor Rising was captured and by the terms of surrender deported to Europe with thirty-six of his followers. The remaining Swedes took an oath of allegiance to the Dutch.[11] Once more the Dutch West India Company was in control of the Delaware River valley.

## Chapter 1 – The City of Amsterdam's Colony

Having incurred large expenses to protect its holdings on the Delaware River, why did the Company turn Fort Casimir over to the City of Amsterdam the year following the conquest and later cede the entire Delaware valley to the City? A number of factors contributed to the decision. The cost of building and maintaining ships and fortresses, paying salaries to the employees in the Company's service in Holland, and salaries plus living expenses to those who came to the New Netherland, were a drain on the Company's treasury. The debt load had been increased by unsuccessful attempts to establish commercial settlements in Brazil and on the Guinea coast of Africa, and by Stuyvesant's two invasions of New Sweden. In short, the Company had overextended itself and did not have sufficient funds to pay its debts to the City.

Throughout the Company's existence the directors were so beset with commercial interests and so eager for financial gain that colonization as an extension of Dutch life and culture was never their aim. They could not conceive of the New Netherland in any way other than for its business potential, and the employees they paid to settle or to farm in the New Netherland were there only to pursue and protect the Company's commerce. Among the employees or "servants" of the Company were skippers of the Company's ships, crew members, Indian traders, commissaries, clerks, cashiers, bookkeepers, artisans, "hired farmers," and many others. All entered into some form of contract to serve the Company for suitable compensation.

During the early years of its existence the Company encouraged *coloniërs* (free colonists) to emigrate to New Netherland and set themselves up on their own account in farming or other permitted occupations. Very little came of this effort because with prosperity in the homeland and religious tolerance there was no strong motivation for Dutchmen to leave their comfortable homes and settle in the American wilderness. A few Walloon families (French-speaking Belgians) came to the New Netherland as *coloniërs* under the auspices of the Company, but this did not result in a flow of Dutch colonists to America.

The growth of a permanent English population in the colonies north and south of the New Netherland provides a sharp contrast with the Company's failure to motivate Dutchmen to come to America. The influx of English colonists, chiefly impelled by religious persecution or poor economic conditions in England, posed a serious threat to the Company. The directors wrote Stuyvesant explaining that one of the reasons why the Delaware colony should be conveyed to the City was "to preserve and guard, without expense to the Company, the Southriver against the invasion and intrusion by the English neighbors on the south [Maryland], of whom for that matter nothing better can be expected, than those on the North...."[12]

Simon Hart wrote about the Company's investments at Fort Casimir and elsewhere on the Delaware: "Plainly the colony had to expand or fail."[13] But the Company had already gotten into financial trouble and could not incur additional expenses. The directors, particularly members of the Amsterdam Chamber, were unwilling to withdraw and allow the English to take over. Of the Company's five chambers, or subsidiary offices, "that place [the Delaware valley] hath been many years under the particular disposition of the Amsterdam Chamber...."[14] The directors of the Amsterdam Chamber had increased the Company's debt when they induced the City to "lease" the vessel *de Wagh* with its 200 men in Stuyvesant's conquest of New Sweden.

Among the twenty directors of the Amsterdam Chamber, a number were active in the City's affairs and could exert influence on the burgomasters. They also pressed the States General to approve the transfer of Company lands to the City.[15] There were other interpersonal relations between City, Company, and States General that time has obscured. If the City could succeed in the Delaware valley where the Company had failed, perhaps the politico-merchants in the Amsterdam Chamber felt that they would eventually benefit, especially since several were also burgomasters of the City. A clause in the agreement with the City stated that if the Company wanted the colony back it could have it within a ten-year period by reimbursing the City for whatever expenses it had incurred with simple interest of 5 percent yearly.[16]

Why did the burgomasters of Amsterdam take over the Delaware colony? How could they justify expending city funds in a venture that had been a serious loss to the Company? One of the reasons is clearly stated in the contemporary records: the government of Amsterdam "hath no intention to extend any authority or power abroad, but merely designs to promote commerce which is the soul of this city...."[17] Clearly the reason given was economic, not political or social.[18] The burgomasters would later learn, however, that the colony's economic success was directly related to political and social factors.

In 1656, Amsterdam, with its population of about 200,000, was the center of Dutch culture and commerce. Sugar, tobacco, and furs were imported from America; silks, porcelain, spices, and other products came from the East Indies on vessels owned by the East India Company. Amsterdam was also dependent on European countries for many commodities. Rye and wheat were largely imported from the Baltic. Oak used in shipbuilding was floated down the Rhine from Western Germany and also loaded on Dutch ships at Bremen and Hamburg, Lübeck and Stettin, Königsberg, and Riga. Fir planks used for ships' decks came from both Norway and the Baltic, and masts were shipped from Norway, Riga, and even Archangel. Pine, which occasionally replaced oak in ship construction, was obtained in Norway and the Baltic. Ship's stores, largely from pines, and other timber extracts, came from Scandinavia and the Baltic lands.[19]

Holland was not an important grain-growing country, nor did she have forests to supply lumber and the straight, tall trees needed for masts and bowsprits in her shipbuilding industry. Amsterdam's reclaimed polders were mostly used as pastureland and to raise vegetables. Since the economy of the City depended upon imports, it made good sense to the burgomasters to control as much as possible the source of needed products. A City-owned New World colony supplying grain and lumber had financial advantages that would relieve the City's entrepreneurs from depending on the Baltic and other European countries. Disruptions in relations with Poland had become a matter of grave importance to the burgomasters, who saw their vital Baltic trade menaced. The development of American sources would protect Amsterdam's economic position.

The Tile House in New Castle, *Robert Montgomery Bird, watercolor, ca. 1826. Nineteenth-century author Robert Montgomery Bird, who grew up in New Castle, created some wonderful views of the town. The Tile House, built on the Strand in the late 1600s and razed in 1884, reflects the Dutch culture of New Castle's earliest citizens.
(Courtesy of Robert Montgomery Bird and The Winterthur Library: Decorative Arts Photographic Collection.)*

## Chapter 1 – The City of Amsterdam's Colony

The burgomasters were satisfied that the climate in the Delaware valley was mild and healthy, and they had been assured that its soil was the richest in the New Netherland, suitable for growing all sorts of crops. The Company had already constructed Fort Casimir, which could serve the City's colony for defense and security, and colonists sent by the City could trade profitably with the neighboring English in Maryland and Virginia as well as with the Indians.[20] The City seemed convinced that ownership rights to the land had been guaranteed since valid deeds in the Company's files had been signed by the Indians.[21] There seemed little doubt "that in case people enough were sent from this country thither, all the products that come at present from the Baltic, masts inculsive, can be raised in New Netherland."[22]

The arrangement for the City to take over the Company's settlement at Fort Casimir (and later a more extensive area) seemed to be mutually advantageous. The proposition was examined and accepted by committees representing the Company and the City, and the City's committee willingly accepted advice from the Company regarding the best way to proceed and make the venture attractive to colonists. The interlocking interests between the City and the Amsterdam Chamber left no doubt that the City would have the Company's full cooperation, and in no sense of the word was any rivalry then anticipated. It was agreed that Petrus Stuyvesant and other Company employees in New Netherland would give their full cooperation to personnel sent by the City, and the City understood that its officials would be beholden to the Company in many ways.

The burgomasters decided that Fort Casimir would be renamed Fort Amstel and the colony called *Nieuwer Amstel* (New Amstel), no doubt named after the village and country district then adjoining Amsterdam. The thirty-six burgomasters selected six of their members to serve as commissioners to handle the affairs of New Amstel, draw up the necessary rules and regulations for its colonization, and act as a sort of board of directors for the infant colony.[23] The "conditions" offered by the City to attract colonists were jointly written by Company and City representatives and publicized in printed leaflets that were widely distributed, not only in Amsterdam but elsewhere in the Netherlands.[24]

The officials of the colony were to be on the City's payroll; these included Jacob Alrichs, a former Company employee with experience in Brazil, as director and commissary general; Martin Krijger (or Crieger), captain of fifty soldiers sent to protect the colonists; and Alexander d'Hinoyossa as his lieutenant. The latter two men had also been in the Company's employ in the New World.[25]

Colonists who agreed to go to New Amstel were not generally employed by the City but were considered individual entrepreneurs. No limit was placed on their potential earnings. The City could buy from them all the grain they raised, the lumber they felled and sawed, the animal pelts they obtained from the Indians, the fish they salted or dried, or any other products marketable in the Netherlands.

The colonists, their families, and their household furniture would be transported at the City's expense, and the colonists would repay the City as their income permitted. Tools and farming implements were to be transported free of charge. The City also agreed to furnish clothing and seed grain for a year and to supply suitable land free of taxes for ten years. The colonists could cut timber without charge to build houses and ships or to sell to the City. Hunting and fishing were also free. If a colonist discovered minerals, crystals, or precious stones he could possess his findings during a term of ten years. After ten years he was obliged to pay the West India Company 10 percent of the proceeds. Thus, the Company, which had heard rumors about gold, silver, and copper mines located in the New Netherland, still had an opportunity for economic profit from the City's colony.

The City would arrange for ships to bring grain, seed, timber, and all other marketable products back to Amsterdam at no cost to the colonists. The City would maintain a warehouse in Amsterdam

## Chapter 1 – The City of Amsterdam's Colony

for the imports from New Amstel. The City would sell that merchandise on behalf of the owner, deducting a commission of 2 percent from all sales and applying 10 percent of the net proceeds to the cost of the colonist's passage to America until such expense was liquidated. The remaining proceeds would be credited to the colonist's account. The City agreed to lay out streets and lots for a town and to divide the land beyond the town into farm fields and pastures. The City would maintain a storehouse at New Amstel stocked with a variety of merchandise that the colonists could purchase on credit at the same prices prevailing in Amsterdam, with one exception. Since the City was obliged to pay customs duties to the Company on both exports and imports into the City's colony, that duty would be added to the price of the merchandise. This is another example of how the Company received benefits from the colony—although it was agreed that customs duties would be used to build and maintain public works in New Netherland as approved jointly by the Company and the City. Finally, a smithy, a wheelwright, a carpenter, a minister, and a schoolmaster would be provided at the City's expense for the convenience and service of the colonists.

The economic incentives were very liberal, and the colonists were also assured of the same administration of justice and the same political rights they enjoyed in the Netherlands. A schout (chief law enforcement officer, in some ways comparable to a sheriff) was to be named by the six commissioners, and three burgomasters for New Amstel were supposed to be appointed by the burghers, or citizens of the town itself. Five or seven schepens (magistrates) were to be selected by the director (Jacob Alrichs) from a list of nominees submitted to him by the burghers. When the town's population reached 200 families, the burghers would elect a council of twenty-one men who would meet the burgomasters and resolve matters relating to the town government.

The schepens were empowered to pronounce sentences in criminal cases and civil suits involving judgments of less than 100 guilders (later increased to 600 guilders).[26] However, a litigant could appeal their decision to a higher court consisting of the director-general (Stuyvesant) and his council sitting in New Amsterdam. This was a curious situation—members of the court of appeals from the City's municipal court were executives in the employ of the West India Company.[27] Since the City paid customs duties to the Company, it would have been an interesting situation if the City found it necessary to appeal to the upper court on a judgment involving such duties!

None of the provisions for setting up a political and judicial organization in the City's colony were ever followed strictly to the letter. In actual practice, the director (first Alrichs and later d'Hinoyossa) set up a council of from three to six members selected from prominent residents who supported their policies. This council functioned as an executive, legislative, and judicial body, although the director held the reins of authority subject to veto by the commissioners in Amsterdam. The distance separating them meant that the director made many decisions without consultation and approval. Stuyvesant and his council did their utmost to keep abreast of what was going on in the City's colony, and because of the close ties between Company and City were able to exercise restraints on Alrichs. As time went on this led to abrasive situations unfair to Alrichs, who had the responsibility for the success of the City's colony but lacked sufficient authority to discharge this responsibility.

It was agreed that the West India Company would continue to retain ownership of Fort Altena (formerly Fort Christina) and maintain a garrison there of Company soldiers. This fort was intended to "awe the natives" and protect the Swedes and Finns living on the Delaware in the Company's territory, who were now Dutch subjects. The garrison usually consisted of from twelve to twenty Dutch soldiers.[28] This too was not desirable, because the City's fort at New Amstel was only six miles distant yet had a different command.

## Chapter 1 – The City of Amsterdam's Colony

Jacob Alrichs left the Netherlands on December 25, 1656, with the first colonists in four vessels. The *Prins Maurits (Prince Maurice)*, the largest, manned by a crew of 16, carried 112 persons, including Alrichs, his wife, 50 soldiers and their officers, Captain Crieger, and Lieutenant d'Hinoyossa. The *Beer (Bear)* conveyed 33 colonists, the *Bever (Beaver)* carried 11, and the *Gelderse Blom (Flower of Guilderland)* also brought 11—a total of 167. The three smaller vessels arrived safely at New Amsterdam enroute to New Amstel, but on March 9, 1657, the *Prins Maurits*, under command of a skipper unfamiliar with American waters, ran aground on Long Island.[29] Eventually, and with considerable difficulty and inconvenience, the director, the colonists, and the soldiers (who marched overland from New Amsterdam) finally converged on New Amstel in the spring of 1657.

Before leaving New Amsterdam, Alrichs received a deed dated April 12, 1657, from Stuyvesant on behalf of the Company that formally conveyed the land at New Amstel to the City. The deed encompassed the land "beginning on the Westside of Minquas or Christina Kil, called in the Indian language Suppeckongh, to the mouth of the bay or river called Boomptjes Hoeck, in the Indian language Canaresse, and as far landward as the boundaries of the Minquas' country...."[30] In terms of modern geography, this included land beginning on the west side of the Christina River at Wilmington (Fort Altena was on the east side of the stream) and extending to Bombay Hook, where the Dutch believed the river ended and Delaware Bay began. Because of imprecise geography the western bounds were vaguely stated. The Minquas, or Susquhannock Indians, controlled land west of the local Lenape's territory, particularly the Susquehanna River and its tributaries, where beavers were numerous.

Alrichs found the fort at New Amstel much decayed and in need of repairs. Twenty families lived in houses they had built near the fort. There were only five or six Dutch families, the remainder being Swedes.[31] After the *Prins Maurits* foundered, only a portion of her cargo could be salvaged before the rough waves tore her apart, and Alrichs lost some of the supplies needed to build and stock a storehouse at New Amstel and to assist the colonists in constructing dwellings. He wrote lengthy letters to the burgomasters in Amsterdam asking for carpenter's tools, nails, oxen, horses, bricks, and other supplies, and he emphasized the need for a minister to conduct church services.[32] He also wrote Stuyvesant for assistance, which was readily given, for Stuyvesant had been impressed that the City's success would contribute to the growth of New Netherland.[33] Stuyvesant, of course, charged the City for any merchandise, livestock, weapons, flour, and the use of vessels that he supplied.

Alrichs' term of service at New Amstel, which lasted a little more than two years, was not a happy one for him. He was hampered by many things beyond his control. The colonists who arrived with him, and those subsequently sent by the City, could not raise enough food to support themselves. Heavy rains in the summers ruined the grain crops and severe winters made life uncomfortable. A general sickness and strange fevers prevailed for two years, taking many lives, including Alrichs' wife who died less than a year after their arrival.[34]

The burgomasters in Amsterdam did not enjoy the profitable imports they expected and were going deeper into debt to support the colony. The City initially raised 36,000 guilders to subsidize the colony, but the need to supply merchandise for the storehouse at New Amstel and to finance ships' voyages necessitated borrowing additional funds from private sources, plus interest.[35] At least 150,000 guilders were invested in the colony, an enormous sum for the times, with negligible returns.[36]

Relations between the Company and the City deteriorated, and Alrichs found himself embroiled in a number of disputes. The Company accused people coming over in the City's ships of smuggling merchandise into New Amstel without paying the required duties. Corrective action was taken by Stuyvesant, who appointed Willem Beeckman, a schepens at New Amsterdam, as commissary

## Chapter 1 – The City of Amsterdam's Colony

and vice-director at Fort Altena on October 28, 1658. In addition to commanding the garrison at the fort, Beeckman was ordered to examine personally all the goods imported and exported at New Amstel to eliminate smuggling.[37] Beeckman was not only expected to audit the import and export duties due the Company, but he was also commander of the Company's soldiers stationed at Fort Altena. Within certain limitations he also had oversight and supervision of the Swedes and Finns living between present-day Wilmington and Philadelphia, but he was cautioned not to disrupt the prior political arrangements Stuyvesant had made after his second attack on New Sweden.[38]

Stuyvesant permitted the Swedes and Finns to enjoy a limited form of self-government by selecting their own sheriff and magistrates, even though they were considered subjects of the Company. But since the Company ceded territory south of Fort Altena to the City, any Swedes or Finns living there became subjects of the City. It was an unusual situation, because there were both language and religious differences between Swedes and Dutch, and the Swedes no longer had political ties with their homeland.

Beeckman, a conscientious Company employee (bringing with him from New Amsterdam his wife and a number of children) encountered numerous problems attendant to his transfer and promotion. He was instructed to be on hand at Fort Altena and also to establish a residence at New Amstel six miles farther south and to enlist the Company's soldiers to inspect the vessels bringing imports to the town. If he found any goods on which duty had not been paid, he was authorized to seize the shipment. It must have seemed to Director Alrichs that his integrity and competence as an employee of the City were being impugned by the Company.

Alrichs, in fact, was doing his utmost to conduct an honest and efficient administration under very trying circumstances. Underlying the apparent harmonious relations between the burgomasters of the City and the directors of the Amsterdam Chamber were differences of opinion and petty jealousies among their respective employees in the New Netherland. Because of Alrichs' determination to enforce strictly the rules governing trade with the Indians and his insistence that the colonists discharge their financial responsibilities to the City, a number of families, including soldiers, fled the colony and settled in Maryland. The ever-present fear that the English might try to seize the colony also was a factor in causing some to leave. The soldiers who fled took with them their wives and children and even maid servants if they had brought them from Amsterdam. Some families also left to reside either on Manhattan Island or in territory under the Company's jurisdiction north of New Amstel. By leaving the City's territory they were able to evade their indebtedness to the City. Because Alrichs did his utmost to halt that exodus from the colony, he was accused of being harsh and inflexible.[39]

Unknown to Alrichs, Stuyvesant was writing letters to the directors of the Amsterdam Chamber about "the deplorable and bad state of affairs in the City's Colony." Whereas the peak population had been about 600 men, women, and children, in a letter dated September 17, 1659, Stuyvesant claimed that New Amstel's population had deteriorated to 30 families and that the 50 soldiers who originally accompanied Alrichs had been reduced by one half.[40]

As a result of Stuyvesant's reports, which must have caused a stir in Amsterdam, Alrichs received a letter dated February 13, 1659, signed by two directors of the Amsterdam Chamber containing a sharp reprimand. He was flatly told that so far as New Amstel was concerned "the Company has reserved for itself supreme authority and supervision. Consequently, the aforesaid colony cannot be considered anything else but a subordinate colony under the aforesaid West India Company...."[41] This, too, must have upset him, because his instructions and financial support came from the City, and the burgomasters were his superiors. Now the Company was clearly indicating that he was expected to serve two masters, which meant subservience to the Company's administrators in New Netherland.

*Chapter 1 – The City of Amsterdam's Colony*

About the same time rumors began to spread in New Amstel that the City's colony was soon to be returned to the Company, making the future look even more uncertain to Alrichs.⁴² Meanwhile, he had again fallen ill from the same unidentified sickness that had taken so many lives and from which he had previously suffered. He died December 30, 1659.

In a clause in his will Alrichs expressed the wish that Lieutenant Alexander d'Hinoyossa should succeed him as director.⁴³ D'Hinoyossa did not wait for the City to get the news of Alrichs' death and name him as his successor; he promptly gave himself the title of president and persuaded members of a new council he appointed to ratify his promotion. He called a meeting of the colonists and read a letter allegedly written by the commissioners stating that the City had resolved to continue to support the colony and never intended to reconvey it to the Company.⁴⁴ Actually the burgomasters did not make this decision until eight months later!⁴⁵

During d'Hinoyossa's self-appointed administration a number of complaints were recorded that accused him of taking advantage of his authority. The wife of one of the soldiers claimed that he confiscated goods belonging to her husband and herself.⁴⁶ Stuyvesant wrote that d'Hinoyossa was haughty and insolent and defamed and slandered his predecessor, the late Director Alrichs.⁴⁷ Willem Beeckman reported that d'Hinoyossa threatened to fine anyone who did not speak well of him.⁴⁸ Of course, Stuyvesant and Beeckman were not impartial in their attitudes toward him, because they were fully aware that he resented any interference from them and wanted as little to do with the Company as possible.

The burgomasters in Amsterdam, and their commissioners, astute businessmen, were familiar with d'Hinoyossa's military record and the favorable reports about his ability that they had received from Alrichs. When they resolved on August 27, 1660, to continue the City's colony and to appoint d'Hinoyossa as the new director and commissary general it left no doubt that they held him in high regard. At the same time they appointed Johan Crato and Gerrit van Sweringen as his assistants and councillors. When d'Hinoyossa opened the letter announcing his official appointment he celebrated by ordering that three shots be fired from the cannon in the fort.[49]

D'Hinoyossa inherited a deteriorating colony that the City had been on the verge of returning to the Company, and his administration should be evaluated in that context. New Amstel was in a desperate financial condition, and it took a firm hand to preserve the colony. D'Hinoyossa took action independent of the West India Company that antagonized Stuyvesant, Beeckman, and the members of Stuyvesant's council at New Amsterdam. When he issued regulations intended to bolster the economy, the Dutch settlers at New Amstel, as well as the Swedes and Finns in the upriver settlements, strongly objected. Nevertheless, he had the support of the burgomasters, and through reports and letters, as well as a personal visit to Amsterdam, he succeeded in convincing the commissioners that the colony could be made profitable to the City.

The records do not clarify whether d'Hinoyossa was responsible for all the measures that were taken, or whether the commissioners also offered suggestions. Since d'Hinoyossa had long experience in the New Netherland, one can assume that he originated the main provisions of the new policy, which can be summarized as follows:[50]

1. The City should take over all of the West India Company's territory along the Delaware River, which would eliminate the Company's activities at Fort Altena, and as far south as the Hoerenkil (present Lewes). Actually the Company was glad to rid itself of this responsibility, and the transaction became official without objection. This gave the City a stronger position against possible English incursions and also gave d'Hinoyossa the Swedes and Finns as subjects, with their 110 boweries, 2,000 cows and oxen, 20 horses, 80 sheep, and several thousand swine.[51] As subjects of the City they could be

## Chapter 1 – The City of Amsterdam's Colony

compelled to sell their surplus grains and other farm products to the City for shipment to Holland, where they would be sold at a profit.

2. Although tobacco, much in demand in Europe, was not raised on the Delaware, it could be obtained at reasonable prices from English planters in nearby Virginia and Maryland and shipped to New Amstel and thence to Holland. Both d'Hinoyossa and van Sweringen had a good rapport with Governor Philip Calvert of Maryland and the tobacco merchants in the province who were eager to sell tobacco to the Dutch and circumvent English duties. This was illegal under the English Navigation Acts, which required the English colonies to ship direct to England and pay whatever duties were applicable to the shipments. Since the Navigation Acts were pri-

*Old Dutch House, Third Street, early 1900s. The Dutch House, built around 1700, is an example of the modest dwellings inhabited by average residents in early New Castle. Restored during the 1930s, it is now a museum of the New Castle Historical Society. (Courtesy of the Horace Deakyne Collection, New Castle Historical Society.)*

marily intended to block Dutch trade directly with the colonies, the traffic between New Amstel and Maryland was considered by English authorities as a form of smuggling.

3. To pay the English for their tobacco the City's colony could supply two products much in demand in Maryland: (a) strong Dutch beer, which was brewed at New Amstel but not in Maryland or Virginia; (b) black slaves to work in the tobacco fields. The slave trade was then practically monopolized by the Dutch, and Negroes seized in Africa could be shipped to New Amstel and then sold to the English. This, too, was a direct violation of the Navigation Acts.

4. Farm laborers from foreign countries, such as Swedes and Finns, should be recruited in large numbers to reinforce the working population in the colony. They were better qualified than Dutch colonists to raise corn, wheat, and rye to be shipped to Amsterdam, and to grow barley and buckwheat for use in brewing beer at New Amstel.

5. The City should make its principal settlement at the head of Appoquinimink Creek (present Odessa, Delaware), where d'Hinoyossa intended to live. Geographically this was an ideal location for trade with the Minquas who came down the Chesapeake in their canoes and could carry their beaver pelts over the short portage that connected the head of Bohemia River with the Appoquinimink. It was also a convenient marketplace to do business with the Maryland merchants who offered to transport 2,000 or 3,000 hogsheads of tobacco annually, if they were supplied with Negroes and other merchandise.[52]

6. Private fur traders should be excluded from the business and the City should exclusively control the fur trade with the Indians to maximize profits.

## Chapter 1 – The City of Amsterdam's Colony

7. Finally, the City's colony should operate independently, and all relations with the West India Company should be minimized. The City should have less connection with the Company and more extensive jurisdiction and authority.[53]

This ambitious program could not be achieved without opposition and criticism. There is little doubt that d'Hinoyossa lacked tact, and his methods were autocratic, which created much resentment in the colony. He was accused of everything from illicitly selling goods belonging to the City to the English for his personal gain to stripping palisades from the fort as firewood for the kettle in which beer was brewed for use in the tobacco trade.[54] When he granted Peter Alrichs (nephew of the late director) the exclusive right to conduct the fur trade with the Indians between Bombay Hook and Cape Henlopen he was accused of showing favoritism.[55] The probability is that he was attempting to monopolize this trade for the City's best interests, as he was supposed to do. Language differences contributed to misunderstandings, and undoubtedly many Swedish and Finnish farmers did not fully understand the reasons for the new policy.

During d'Hinoyossa's administration the population increased by the influx of both Dutch families and "foreign" farm workers. Among the newcomers was Peter Cornelis Plockhoy, a Mennonite from Zieriksee, who brought forty-one persons in July of 1663 on the *Sint Jacob (Saint Jacob)* to form a semisocialistic community at Lewes.[56] The same vessel discharged sixty farm laborers and girls, with farm implements, at New Amstel. D'Hinoyossa himself brought 150 people (including thirty-two Finns) when he returned from a voyage to Amsterdam in 1663.[57]

In the months that followed quantities of furs, grains, tobacco, timber, and other products were shipped to Amsterdam from the Delaware colony. At long last the venture was beginning to pay off, and the future looked bright.

D'Hinoyossa has been accused of seeking personal gain at the expense of the City in this renaissance of the colony, and there is little doubt that he was motivated by self-interest.[58] The same thing, however, can be said about Schout van Sweringen and the commissioners of the City's colony back in Amsterdam. Once the colony began to prosper, many of the burgomasters invested their own private funds in the New Amstel commerce. In the latter days of d'Hinoyossa's administration, the City itself handled only one-quarter of the shipments from the Delaware colony, whereas individual burgomasters conducted the majority of the business on a personal basis.[59] According to the business ethics of the times, apparently there was nothing wrong in giving this concrete evidence of the confidence the Dutch politico-merchants had in the prospering colony.

All hope for the continuing success of the City's colony came to a sudden halt on October 1, 1664, when Sir Robert Carr, in the service of the Duke of York, sailed up the Delaware River and attacked New Amstel with a superior military force. What had happened was that Charles II, urged by Parliament, concluded that it was to England's economic interests to possess the New Netherland and eliminate the Dutch competition for furs, tobacco, grain, lumber, and other New World products. England was suffering from Dutch commerce, which reduced the English colonial trade and menaced economic expansion in America.

On March 12, 1664, the king granted his brother James Stuart, Duke of York (later to become James II), a patent that included all of the New Netherland except the land on the western shore of the Delaware River where the City of Amsterdam's colony was flourishing. As has been explained, Lord Baltimore considered this territory part of Maryland according to his proprietary grant from Charles I, the father of Charles II. How could Charles II, or his brother James, legally confiscate land that their father had patented to Lord Baltimore? It was now well known, however, that Maryland merchants were enjoying a lucrative but illicit business with the Dutch

## Chapter 1 – The City of Amsterdam's Colony

in the City's colony and that the Maryland government chose not to disturb this commerce by a confrontation with the Dutch over ownership of the territory.

Stuyvesant surrendered Fort Amsterdam and Manhattan Island to the Duke of York's warships and troops, giving the English control of the heart of New Netherland. Although the Duke's instructions to his officials said nothing about New Amstel, it was immediately apparent that their mission would be futile unless they put a stop to the commerce between the City's colony and Maryland. To Sir Robert Carr was delegated the task of invading the City's colony even though control by the Duke of York would be inimical to the best commercial interests of the Province of Maryland. The nuances should not be overlooked because even after the attack Maryland officials continued to be friendly to the Dutch officials, although an English government was ruling the former Dutch colony on land claimed by Lord Baltimore.

D'Hinoyossa ordered the garrison in the fort to resist, but the English attackers overran the stronghold and confiscated all the merchandise and livestock owned by the City. The loot included 100 sheep, 30 or 40 horses, 50 or 60 cows and oxen, 60 to 70 black slaves, a brewhouse, a distillery, a sawmill, plows and farm tools, arms, powder, shot, 24 cannon, and quantities of corn and hay that had recently been harvested. D'Hinoyossa's estate and personal property and Negro slaves were lost to the enemy, and he and Schout van Sweringen and their families fled to Maryland to seek haven among their English friends there.[60] In addition, Carr sent a boat to the Plockhoy settlement at Lewes, where his soldiers pillaged the homes of the Dutch Mennonites.

New Amstel, now under the rule of the Duke of York's new government, with Colonel Richard Nicolls as the deputy governor, was given a new name—New Castle. The surrender terms were more generous than the residents had reason to expect from an invading force. The Dutch, Swedish, Finnish, and other alien farmers and craftsmen were allowed to retain their homes and personal property. Those who did not want to live under the Duke of York's rule were free to depart unmolested and to take their personal property with them. The others took this oath of allegiance:

> I doe sweare by the Almighty God that I will beare faith and allegiance to his Majesty of great Brittaine, and that I will obey all such commands as I shall receive from the Governor, Deputy Governor, or other officers appointed by his Majesty's authority soe long as I live in these or any other His Majesty's Territoryes.

After taking the oath they were as free as native Englishmen to enjoy the privileges of English citizenship and liberty of conscience in church disciplines. The Dutch magistrates were permitted to remain in office subject to the authority of the Duke of York's government.

---

[1] Approval was given by the States General, the governing body of the United Netherlands, after discussions were carried on over several months *(Documents Relative to the Colonial History of the State of New York*, ed. E. B. O'Callaghan, 15 vols. [Albany, 1856], I, 637 [hereafter cited as NYCD]).

[2] NYCD, I, 642–43.

[3] NYCD, XII, 449, cf. XII, 443. (This volume was edited by Berthold Fernow.)

[4] The classic account of early Swedish colonization is Amandus Johnson, *The Swedish Settlements on the Delaware*, 2 vols. (New York, 1911). Reliable secondary sources are H. Clay Reed, *The Delaware Colony* (New York, 1970); *Readings in Delaware History*, ed. Carol E. Hoffecker (Newark, Del., 1973); Carol E. Hoffecker, *Delaware: A Bicentennial History* (New York, 1977); and John Munroe, *Colonial Delaware* (Millwood, N.Y., 1978). The present writer's volumes on the Dutch and English are cited below.

[5] The history and politics of the West India Company are fully discussed in Thomas J. Condon, *New York Beginnings, the Commercial Origins of New Netherland* (New York, 1968) and Van Cleaf Bachman, *Peltries or Plantations, the Economic Policies of the Dutch West India Company in New Netherland, 1623–1639* (Baltimore, 1969).

[6] Although Swanendael was the first Dutch settlement in Delaware, the West India Company had earlier made a short-lived settlement on Burlington Island and built Fort Nassau at Gloucester, N.J. See C. A. Weslager, *Dutch*

## Chapter 1 – The City of Amsterdam's Colony

*Explorers, Traders and Settlers in the Delaware Valley* (Philadelphia, 1961), chap. 2 and 3. The account of Swanendael and supporting documentation is found in chap. 4.

[7] *Dutch Explorers*, 285. See also C. A. Weslager, "Who Survived the Indian Massacre at Swanendael?" *de Halve Maen*, 40 (1965): 9–10.

[8] C. A. Weslager, *The English on the Delaware* (New Brunswick, N.J., 1967).

[9] Dudley Lunt, *The Bounds of Delaware* (Wilmington, 1947).

[10] Weslager, *Dutch Explorers*, 152–56.

[11] "Relation of the Surrender of New Sweden, by Governor Johan Clason Rising, 1655," *Narratives of Early Pennsylvania, West New Jersey and Delaware*, ed. Albert Cook Myers (New York, 1912), 170–76. See also Johnson, *Swedish Settlements*, I, 591–616.

[12] NYCD, XII, 443.

[13] Simon Hart, "The City–Colony of New Amstel on the Delaware: I," *de Halve Maen*, 39 (1965): 8. The second part of Hart's article appears in *ibid.*, 40 (1965): 7–8.

[14] NYCD, I, 627.

[15] NYCD, I, 629.

[16] NYCD, I, 630.

[17] NYCD, I, 630.

[18] The Company suggested three different sites to the burgomasters, and Fort Casimir was their choice (Hart, "The City-Colony: I," 6).

[19] Bachman, *Peltries or Plantations*, 63.

[20] NYCD, I, 612–13.

[21] NYCD, I, 614. The fact that the Assembly of XIX, the Company's executive committee, as well as the Estates General, approved the transaction facilitated the negotiations of the Amsterdam Chamber.

[22] NYCD, I, 614.

[23] NYCD, XII, 133. The name New Amstel was agreed upon in Amsterdam in 1656 before the colony was actually settled. The names of the six original commissioners are given by Hart in "The City-Colony: I," 6.

[24] NYCD, XII, 131.

[25] NYCD, XII, 132, 163. The soldiers, also paid by the City, were intended for defense against the Indians and as a police patrol for law enforcement (*ibid.*, 273). The salaries of soldiers and officers are given in *ibid.*, I, 641.

[26] It is impossible to equate the buying power of a guilder in the seventeenth century with a modern inflated American dollar with any degree of accuracy. Van Laer wrote in 1908 that the seventeenth-century guilder was worth 40

cents and a stuiver 2 cents (*Van Rensselar Bowier Manuscripts*, trans. and ed. A. J. F. Van Laer [Albany, 1908], 847). In 1965 it was estimated that the seventeenth-century guilder was equivalent in buying power to $10.50 (Hart, "The City-Colony: II,"13). See also Richard H. Amerman, "Trip to America Costly in 1662," *de Halve Maen*, 38 (1963), 14, 16. Dr. Charles T. Gehring states that he has wrestled with the problem of the value of the guilder and that it can only be approached in terms of salaries contrasted with the price of goods. When asked this question he says, "I usually say that a horse was worth c. 200 guilders and would be the equivalent to owning a Mercedes" (personal letter, March 2, 1982). On the basis of executive salaries, Jacob Alrichs was paid a salary of 100 guilders a month and 300 guilders a year for expenses (NYCD, II, 169). As an army captain, Martin Crieger's salary was 50 guilders a month and 150 guilders a year for rations. The schout received 40 guilders a month salary and 150 guilders a year to cover his board.

27 A translation of the conditions is given in NYCD, I, 630–35. There was also a second set of regulations governing the conduct of the colonists during their period aboard a ship enroute to New Netherland. Since some were transported on vessels belonging to the City, others on Company-owned vessels, and still others on vessels chartered by private owners, the commissioners wanted uniform regulations observed. See *New York Historical Manuscripts: Dutch, Delaware Papers (Dutch Period)*, ed. Charles T. Gehring (Baltimore, 1981), 84–97. We learn from the latter conditions that the colonists were bound to remain at New Amstel for at least four years unless the Director and his council permitted them to leave at an earlier date.

28 NYCD, XII, 132, 176.

29 NYCD, XII, 163–65.

30 NYCD, XII, 7, 166. This was the same land Stuyvesant received from the Lenape chiefs, July 9, 1651, during his second invasion of New Sweden.

31 NYCD, II, 17. As of August 16, 1659, Alrichs said that 110 houses were built, which must have included both residential and nonresidential structures (*ibid.*, 69).

32 NYCD, XII, 173, 199. There was no minister in the first expedition.

33 NYCD, XII, 185. The Company was obligated to protect the City's colony, particularly against any efforts of the English to seize the territory (*ibid.*, 260, 273). The general concept mutually understood was that the land the Company deeded to the City was unencumbered, and if another party or nation claimed it, the Company was responsible for protecting the City's ownership. If the Company failed to do so the City had the right to demand damages for any losses it sustained.

34 The many problems Alrichs faced are enumerated in numerous letters to Stuyvesant and others of which those in NYCD, XII, 236, 249 are typical. For

the details of some of his building activities at New Amstel, see Weslager, *Dutch Explorers,* 194–213. Jeannette Eckman gives an accurate if somewhat simplistic summary of Alrichs' activities in *New Castle on the Delaware* (New Castle, 1950), 28–31.

[35] Some of the City's borrowings are enumerated in NYCD, II, 2, 4, 12, 17, 48, 56, 101.

[36] Hart, "The City-Colony: I," 13.

[37] NYCD, XII, 219. The imported goods were stamped in Holland with the Company's mark after the duty was paid (*ibid.,* 212). Merchandise shipped from New Amstel on which duty was paid was similarly marked.

[38] Instructions to Beeckman are given in NYCD, XII, 220–21. In *Crane Hook on the Delaware* (Newark, Del., 1958), chap. 3, Jeannette Eckman discusses the relationship between the denationalized Swedish colonists and the administrations of the City and the Company.

[39] NYCD, XII, 249.

[40] NYCD, XII, 254, 288. Following are the names as of June 25, 1659, of six enlisted soldiers who deserted the colony and fled to Maryland: Hans Roeloff from Stockholm, Sweden; Andries Thomasen from Jutland, Denmark; Cornelis Jurriaensen from Winseren, Sweden; Jacob Jansz from Antwerp (present Belgium); and two Dutchmen, Jan Hinger from Utrecht, and Evert Brants from Amersfort (*ibid.,* II, 64).

[41] Gehring, *New York Historical Manuscripts,* 136. Fernow's translation of this letter in NYCD, XII, 233–34, differs from Dr. Gehring's. Where translations of the same documents appear in both sources, the writer prefers to use direct quotations from Gehring, a professional linguist, better qualified to translate seventeenth-century Dutch than Fernow, whose native language was neither English nor Dutch.

[42] NYCD, II, 78. The burgomasters decided on September 30, 1659, that since the colony was so costly it should be surrendered to the West India Company and that negotiations with the directors of the Amsterdam Chamber should be undertaken. Stuyvesant opposed the Company taking back the colony, which he felt would be too costly to rejuvenate and maintain after a period of mismanagement (*ibid.,* XII, 327).

[43] NYCD, XII, 289.

[44] NYCD, XII, 322.

[45] NYCD, XII, 333.

[46] The complaint of Sergeant Willem van Diemen's wife appears in a letter, NYCD, XII, 329–30.

[47] NYCD, XII, 290, 332.

[48] NYCD, XII, 335.

[49] NYCD, XII, 333.

[50] Some of the discussions wherein the burgomasters and the Amsterdam Chamber agreed on a new policy are recorded in NYCD, II, 196–216.

[51] NYCD, II, 210. To Alrichs's credit, it should be said that during his administration he raised the question of the desirability of all the territory coming under the City's authority (*ibid.*, 18–19).

[52] NYCD, XII, 450. Augustine Herrman, who owned Bohemia Manor at the head of Bohemia River, planned to build a cartroad from his manor to the Appoquinimink to facilitate the shipment of merchandise over the Indian portage path (*ibid.*, 337). See also Gehring, *New York Historical Manuscripts*, 243.

[53] NYCD, II, 200.

[54] NYCD, XII, 375, 379. He was also accused of selling the City's millstones to the English for 1,000 pounds of tobacco for his own personal gain (*ibid.*, 379).

[55] NYCD, XII, 368. Later Alrichs was given the exclusive right to the Indian fur trade at New Amstel in behalf of the City. Another City employee handled the Indian trade at the Hoerenkil and a third at Passayunk, an Indian settlement within the bounds of present Philadelphia (*ibid.*, 450).

[56] Plockhoy's contract with the burgomasters was dated June 9, 1662 (Leland Harder, "Plockhoy and His Settlement at Zwanendael," *Delaware History*, 3 [1949]: 138–154). On September 19, 1913, the Netherlands Society of Philadelphia placed a memorial plaque to Plockhoy in the town hall at Zierikzee. The inscription erroneously states he was "founder of the Dutch Colony at Swaanendael, Delaware, U.S.A." As pointed out above, the ill-fated colony was founded in 1631 by Dutch patroons three decades before Plockhoy's voyage.

[57] NYCD, XII, 447.

[58] Weslager, *Dutch Explorers*, 242–43.

[59] Hart, "The City-Colony: II," 7.

[60] Weslager, *English on the Delaware*, chap. 12. The Dutch recaptured the Delaware colony (and the rest of New Netherland) in 1673, but by the treaty of Westminster the following year the territory was restored to the English (*ibid.*, chap. 13). Information about the plunder seized by the English at New Amstel is found in Gerrit van Sweringen's deposition dated May 12, 1684, made when he was 84 years of age and still living in Saint Mary's, Maryland (NYCD, III, 345–46). Van Sweringen, his wife Barbara De Barrette and his two children, Elizabeth and Zacharias, both born in New Amstel, became citizens of Maryland in 1669 (*Maryland Archives*, II, 205).

Scharf wrote that d'Hinoyossa was vice-director at New Amstel from

## Chapter 1 – The City of Amsterdam's Colony

1659 to 1663, and "upon his retirement from the position he obtained possession of a large tract of land at Appoquinimink (Odessa) where he signified his intention to reside and engage in trading. He was settled at his plantation but a few months when a change in affairs gave the territory to the British, and his estate was confiscated and granted to Captain Edmund Cantwell in about 1676" (Scharf, II, 1005). Sally Schwartz cited Scharf for her statement that "d'Hinoyossa received the first known land grant in the area [Odessa]" ("Cantwell's Bridge, Delaware: A Demographic and Community Study," *Delaware History,* 19 [Spring-Summer, 1980], 20). The writer has failed to find evidence that d'Hinoyossa had a land grant at present-day Odessa or that he lived there. Moreover, he was still the director on October 1, 1664, when Sir Robert Carr attacked New Amstel.

# Voices and Viewpoints

*The Reverend George Ross, the first rector of Immanuel Church, corresponded regularly with the Society for the Propagation of the Gospel in Foreign Parts, the Church of England missionary agency that sent him to Delaware. In 1727, he submitted a history of his church that included a great deal of information on the town. Twenty some years later he pithily expressed the relationship between New Castle, already nearly a century old, and Wilmington, the new town in the area.*

# The Reverend George Ross

*Excerpts from*
*"Mr. Ross's History of his Church At New Castle," March 1, 1727*

In the said three counties, New Castle is the chief and best Town, & most commodiously situated for Trade and Navigation. It stands upon a pleasant eminence, and is found, of late years, to be both healthy and agreeable, & in summer is preferable to any upon Delaware, for its coole and refreshing breezes—an advantage it owes to its being nearer the sea, by 40 miles, than the so much talked of Philadelphia.

....

In the year 1703, those in New Castle of the Communion of the Church of England, from a sense of a want of a Person in Holy Orders to reside among them, & observing how the Presbyterians were gaining ground in the place, by reason of their having a Preacher to promote their interest, Resolved to Petition the Bishop of London to take compassion on their deplorable circumstances, which resolution they put in practice the Eleventh of August, in the said year, & in confidence of a favorable answer from his Lordship's charitable disposition, they agreed with Workmen to build a House of public Worship.

....

In the middle of the Town lies a spacious Green, in the form of a Square, in a corner whereof stood formerly a Fort, & on the Ground whereon the said Citadel was built, they agreed to erect their church, from a persuasion that, as it belonged to their Sovereign, it was not in the power of any of their troublesome Neighbors to disturb them in their commendable undertaking. In the year 1704, Emanuel Church, at New Castle, was founded, & by the charitable contributions of several Gent[n] in Pennsylvania, as well as by the large collections of Inhabitants of New Castle—not only Churchmen but Presbyterians—it was finished and opened 1706.

....

The number of Inhabitants belonging to this Church, or usually frequenting at first, was about 20 Families, which, allowing three to a Family, to attend Divine Worship, amounts to three score. They were generally low in their condition, but not indigent, having wherewithal to support themselves, but little to spare. The employ & business of such of them as lived in the Town was retailing of Goods, Rum, Sugar & Molasses, together with some European Goods. Some enjoyed Posts in the Government, & others get their living by their handy crafts, as Carpenters, Smiths & Shoe Makers. Those of them that had their residence in the Country were occupied in clearing & grubbing of Land, in raising of Grain, as Wheat, Rye, Indian Corn, Oats & Barley; in improving their Stock, such as Horses, Horn Cattle, Sheep & Hogs. Few or none of them had Estates to support them without being obliged to their Trade Labour & Industry. Their sentiments in matters of Religion—I mean of those who were my first hearers—were pretty uniform, & framed upon Church principles. Most of them lived together, like Towns in England, while others, who manured the Ground, lived dispersed up & down a large compass of Ground, all of them so far distant from any other church that the healthiest and strongest among them could not, without great application & going on Horseback, attend Divine Service there.

....

The present number of inhabitants, professing themselves members of the Church under my care, are about 100 Families, & most of them much improved in their Fortunes & condition, having for the number of People as great plenty of Bread & provisions of all sorts, as Beef, Pork, Veal, Mutton & Dung Hill Fowl, as most other parts have in the King's Dominions, either at home or abroad.[1]

## *From George Ross to the Reverend Doctor Bearcroft, March 27, 1750*

The town of Newcastle consisting of about fourscore houses waxes poorer & poorer, And falls into Contempt more and more, every year, haveing Several houses without inhabitant, & Some not fit for habitation. The

Church under my care, visibly Shareing in the wretched Fate of the poor town, makes a much meaner appearance now than at any time heretofore. This dying Condition is partly owing to an upstart village lying on a Neighbouring creek, which yields a convenient port to the adjacent Country. And here I cannot but bewail my own Scituation, that I am fix'd in a place, whence I cannot transmitt a more Satisfactory Account of my Stewardship. I do my endeavour with the help of God, to behave myself unblameably, and to discharge my duty both publickly and privately as upon other accounts, so with this view, that no man may upbraid me with haveing on hand in the languishing State of this Church.[2]

[1] William Stevens Perry, ed., *Historical Collections Relating to the American Episcopal Church,* 5 vols. (Hartford, Conn., 1878), 5: 43–46.

[2] Ross to Bearcroft, March 27, 1750, Series B, Volume 18, p. 154, Henry Clay Reed, Transcripts of Delaware Extracts from the Papers of the Society for the Propagation of the Gospel, University of Delaware Library, Newark, Delaware.

## Chapter Two

After its ethnically and religiously diverse beginning, New Castle developed into a town in which English culture, politics, and economic connections dominated. This article is drawn from the author's dissertation, "Anglicization in a 'Frenchified, Scotchified, Dutchified Place': New Castle, Delaware, 1690–1750" (Ph.D. dissertation, New York University, 1994).

## Great Expectations, Practical Accomplishments: New Castle, 1700–1750

*William R. Cario*

When Doctor Benjamin Bullivant passed through New Castle, Delaware, in 1697, his travel notes captured both the past and potential future of the community. His seventeenth-century gaze centered on the town's buildings, "the Customs house[,] a small Ruinated church[,] a prettey town house…, they have six guns mounted on ye bank but hardly enough to command the River." These few phrases hint at the condition of the leading seventeenth-century town on the Delaware River as it was poised to enter the next century. The doctor recognized two somewhat conflicting aspects of the town. While New Castle had already endured a series of owners and several waves of inhabitants in its forty-year history, Bullivant detected a sense of newness and opportunity in the community. The ruined church and inadequate defenses were signs of disorder, yet the government buildings constructed in the past ten years, the customs house and the assembly hall that he called a town house, indicated energy and enterprise. His journal intimates that New Castle in 1700 was on the brink of a changing order.[1]

Indeed, in the first half of the eighteenth century, New Castle residents strove to find an economic niche for their town and to foster community institutions—especially churches—in a remarkably diverse setting. Many of their hopes did not come to fruition; before 1750 Philadelphia and Wilmington surpassed the older town in economic and political power. Nevertheless, the New Castle residents' actions laid the groundwork for long-term development. Their improvement of New Castle's physical surroundings, their assertion of New Castle's significance in the Lower Counties, and their willingness to form congregations in a setting of diversity and tolerance gave the town an opportunity to survive through a difficult century.

## New Castle In 1700

New Castle's location was attractive to early settlers. Because the Delaware River made a bend there, the current slowed and the river itself narrowed, providing the town with an opportunity to control access upstream. The course of the river bequeathed a somewhat small but useful port for ships. It also provided the first potable water for people arriving into the Delaware Valley and the last water for ships leaving on the long journey across the Atlantic. In 1700 it was considered one of the four preeminent market towns on the Delaware, with shipbuilding facilities, a brickyard, lumberyard, tannery, breweries, and a number of thriving inns. The customs house supervised trade entering the Delaware from abroad and attempted to regulate it. New Castle served as an important crossroads for goods, people, and mail traveling between colonies or across the ocean.

The face of the town was oriented east toward the Delaware River. The greatest concentration of people in New Castle County—

*Chapter 2 – Great Expectations, Practical Accomplishments*

perhaps up to 50 percent—lived in and around town. Of the approximately 115 families who inhabited New Castle Hundred, the vast majority of at least 80 families lived in town, making its population approximately 350 to 400 people. The structure of the town, based on the grid pattern established by the Dutch, reflected the overwhelming influence of the river. By 1700, merchants were building homes, storehouses, and wharves on the riverbank; a second row of homes provided housing for the slightly less fortunate who could not afford riverfront property. Behind those homes lay the town green on which were located the courthouse, a customs house, and the ruins of an old fort. Homes and an old dilapidated church faced the green, while on several streets behind the green were scattered houses. The town commons lay to the south and southwest of town, descending into swampland; at the northern end of town near the river was an old mill. New Castle boasted of a brickyard, several inns, a lumberyard, a small shipworks, some breweries, and several warehouses for European merchant families, along with the usual assortment of smiths, shoemakers, ropemakers, and carpenters. What it lacked was also significant: there were no Christian churches, the old Reformed congregation building just off the green having been virtually abandoned. Neither was there a school building.[2]

An examination of the tax assessment records of New Castle County for 1693 and 1697 gives a distinct sense of the composition of New Castle's population by 1700. Although a significant portion of the population was not British, the English and their cousins were well on their way towards dominating the Delaware landscape. After thirty-five years of English authority, the New Castle County assessment lists showed that over one-third of the names were still non-British, mostly Dutch and Swedish, with a scattering of French and German. In New Castle Hundred, the total of non-British names in the 1697 assessment constituted a higher percentage of the population—41 percent—than any other hundred in the county. The actual percentage of people from non-British backgrounds is most likely higher than the figures above indicate because some residents had already begun to anglicize their names. For example, Thomas Janvier was also known as January, and John William Neering, whose family had already anglicized his sur- and middle names, dropped his last name altogether to make it more British-sounding.[3]

The growing British population of New Castle around 1700 contrasts starkly with another colonial river town of somewhat similar history. Albany, New York, was able to retain its Dutch culture and influence much longer into the eighteenth century because of its location and its small, homogeneous nucleus of Dutch leaders. Whereas in 1697, 59 percent of New Castle's household heads had English names, only 7 percent of Albany's household heads did. A number of English settlers took Dutch names to fit into the prevailing order; at the same time, New Castle's non-English residents were taking English names for a similar reason. While Albany was clinging to its Dutch roots in 1700, New Castle's community was taking on a more diverse cast.[4]

At the turn of the century, into that quite pluralistic population, a significant few newcomers to New Castle, English and Scotsmen of relatively wealthy means, settled in or near town. Among others, Bryan MacDonald moved his family from Scotland to New Castle County in the 1680s to take advantage of Penn's offer of land. George Dakeyne brought his surveying skills to Delaware from the eastern side of the river in the decade before 1700, while Jaspar Yeates slowly moved his possessions and interests from the West Indies by way of Pennsylvania after 1700. Hercules and James Coutts established a trading factory for their family mercantile network in town before 1700. Richard Halliwell bought farmland in New Castle County during the first twenty years of William Penn's control of the Delaware Valley. Robert French moved his family and possessions north from Kent County to New Castle, while his relative John French took residence in town by 1700. The Reverend George Ross left a chaplain-

*Chapter 2 – Great Expectations, Practical Accomplishments*

cy in the Royal Navy to take a missionary position in New Castle's Anglican church in 1703.⁵

It was these recent immigrants to northern Delaware, and others like them, who came to dominate New Castle for the next thirty years. The town's future leaders were not a homogeneous group like the Quakers who dominated Pennsylvania. Neither did they have a deliberate plan to settle and dominate the region. They had not known each other before meeting in the Delaware Valley, nor did they arrive in the region bound by family, religion, community, or vision. An emerging, though still inchoate, sense of empire and economic opportunity drew them to the town. Several settled in New Castle because of the access it afforded them to other parts of the empire, especially the Chesapeake and the West Indies. The town had a reputation for flaunting the Navigation Acts and attracting

*New Castle County Courthouse, ca. 1940s. The central portion was built in 1732, replacing a building from the 1680s that had burned in 1729. The wings are later additions.*
*(Courtesy of the Horace Deakyne Collection, New Castle Historical Society.)*

entrepreneurs who skirted the law. The chief royal officer on the river reported in 1698 that a Scots-owned ship carrying £1000 of pirate-purloined East Indies goods stopped at New Castle where the customs collector accepted a bribe of five barrels of goods to let the ship pass. William Penn accused Jaspar Yeates of involvement in the illegal trade with Curacao. Richard Halliwell, John Donaldson, William Howston, Robert French, and James and Hercules Coutts took advantage of royal laxity to participate in the tobacco trade, exchanging manufactured goods for tobacco in Delaware and on the Elk, Sassafras, and Bohemia rivers of Maryland's Eastern Shore. To avoid detection and taxes, they portaged the tobacco forty miles to the Delaware River "at a place a little below Newcastle called Bumbo Hook," from which they shipped the contraband to Scotland or the West Indies. As an official complained in 1701, almost all the Lower Counties trade "is engrossed by the Scotch."[6]

A number of residents settled in New Castle because of formal and informal ties to imperial authority. Despite his involvement in the illegal tobacco trade, John Donaldson was appointed a county justice of the peace by Delaware's only royal governor. Jaspar Yeates's connections with Robert Quary, royal vice-admiralty judge for the Delaware River, were quite close; he informed Quary of a contraband-laden ship in New Castle in 1698. In the early eighteenth century Yeates decided to throw in his lot with New Castle rather than Philadelphia, perhaps because of his royalist connections. Quary suggested in 1702 that if Queen Anne made Delaware a royal colony, she could name Yeates governor, "impowering him to preserve the peace of the Province." Even those who consistently violated the Navigation Acts turned to the crown when King William's War put New Castle at some risk from French and Spanish privateers. When the Quaker leaders showed little inclination to defend the Delaware shoreline, such traders petitioned the empire for help. Individuals with more formal ties to imperial rule later appeared in town. Samuel Lowman was appointed royal customs collector in 1703, and George

*Chapter 2 – Great Expectations, Practical Accomplishments*

Ross, missionary of the Society for the Propagation of the Gospel, arrived a year later.[7]

### Remaking New Castle

In August 1706, many New Castle residents attended the consecration of a new church in town. They listened to the Reverend Andreas Rudman, a local Lutheran pastor, preach the initial sermon to a congregation of visitors and local residents, including the recently arrived pastor of the Anglican congregation, George Ross. The edifice on the northeast corner of New Castle's green was one of the institutions, along with the new Quaker and Presbyterian meeting houses under construction, which lent a more British cast to the town's polyglot character. The colonial statehouse seated the Lower Counties Assembly, which had split off from the Pennsylvania Assembly in 1704. New Castle's waterfront was developing in anticipation of competition with Philadelphia for economic dominance of the region. Indeed, after 1700 New Castle began to take quite a different direction from its rather somnolent seventeenth-century style.

New Castle's newer residents staked their economic hopes on the town, buying up most of the available lots. The county records of warrants and surveys show that of the twenty-eight people who bought town lots in New Castle between 1690 and 1708, twenty had arrived in the region after 1690. Sixteen buyers of town lots were of the Anglican faith, the most prominent of whom, Robert French, Joseph Wood, and Richard Halliwell, purchased several properties.

These entrepreneurs also provided the impetus to reshape the physical spaces in and around New Castle, an effort that interested few others in the region. Most Delaware settlers inhabited the fertile northern or southern reaches of New Castle County along the Christiana, Brandywine, or Appoquinimink creeks, far away from the swampy environs surrounding the town. The town's new leaders, however, initiated nearly all of the twelve requests for survey or resurvey of tracts in New Castle Hundred extant for the period 1690 to

1708. Robert French received two tracts, John Donaldson purchased three tracts before his death in 1702, Richard Halliwell owned large tracts in the area surrounding New Castle, and William Howston purchased two parcels of land in 1701. That same year, James Claypoole asked for a resurvey of 200 acres he was planning to buy in New Castle Hundred. Claypoole, a merchant as well as Donaldson's co-county registrar of wills and deeds, in 1703 rejected his Quaker faith to experience a deathbed baptism by George Keith, the Quaker-turned-Anglican missionary.[8]

Why were these men interested in the relatively worthless marshland surrounding New Castle? To be sure, the marshlands provided resources such as firewood and small game. Of greater importance, the marshes determined the physical size and shape of New Castle. Since the 1650s residents had erected dikes to enlarge the area into which the lowland town could spread. Control of the dikes determined the extent of the physical growth of New Castle and their upkeep helped constrain the environment of the town, which had a swamp-infested reputation. Under the Duke of York, town government had overseen the upkeep of the dikes, but with proprietary rule the county and provincial governments had somewhat neglected them. There is some evidence that several of the leading Anglicans in town were attempting to gain authority over the marshes to control flooding. In 1701 John Donaldson, Richard Halliwell, and Robert French contracted to buy a marsh in which was situated the broad dike that confined the wetland on the northeast side of town. As a civic duty these three men took over responsibility for the maintenance of that dike.[9]

There is another piece of evidence that New Castle's newcomers attempted to take control of the town's physical assets. In 1703 Halliwell led a group of New Castle residents to apply for control of the town commons. While under the Duke of York town leaders regulated the commons, after 1682—with the demise of town government—county officials had ignored such town matters. Halliwell and

## Chapter 2 – Great Expectations, Practical Accomplishments

his associates were willing to oversee the management of the town commons and nearby dikes in order to retain control of nearby resources.[10]

There are several indications that New Castle served as a significant seaport until 1710. While a minister on his first trip to town in 1708 described it as "formerly a place of great Trade," he also noticed several ships in port and a large percentage of the town's population in pursuit of mercantile interests. In 1701, William Penn accused Jaspar Yeates of being a major trafficker in the illegal trade with Curacao. Early in the decade, the Coutts family, using New Castle as a base, took advantage of hostilities with France to capture enemy merchantmen. The records of a New Castle carpenter show that during the first decade of the century, he constructed ships for several of the merchants, including Coutts and French. Traders with Scotch connections competed with Philadelphia merchants for trade with the West Indies. James Coutts was most likely a factor for his family interests in the New World; as such he owned ships that regularly crossed the Atlantic. Even Penn acknowledged to his lieutenant governor that these new immigrants "have made New Castle so Considerable" an economic power.[11]

Finally, the New Castle gentry were in the forefront of their community's attempt to establish—and in one case, reestablish—houses of worship in town. According to Immanuel Church tradition, Anglicans had started meeting together in town by 1689. Throughout the next decade there was little attempt to do more than gather in people's homes for worship and wait for traveling clergy to minister to their needs. Some familiar persons provided leadership for the new church as the activities of the Anglican congregation increased early in the eighteenth century. Halliwell, Wood, and Yeates were overseers of the building process, collecting funds for a church edifice from 1703 on. The congregation had applied to the Society for the Propagation of the Gospel (SPG) for a pastor by that same year and might also have elected church wardens. The brick walls of the church rose and the windows had arrived by October 1704; when George Ross landed in September 1705, construction was almost finished.[12]

The completed edifice, a brick building with a cedar roof, fifty feet long and thirty feet wide, located on the village green, clearly represented the church's ties with England. With two doors and five glass windows, including a large round window at the east end of the church, it was one of the most noticeable buildings in town. Neither its size nor its accoutrements matched the early Anglican churches in Boston and New York. It lacked an organ, clock, and lighting that might have shown off the wealth of the community. Nevertheless, the royal coat of arms on the wall and the communion set donated by Queen Anne distinguished Immanuel Church from other New Castle structures. Not even the courthouse showed as many overtly royal symbols.[13]

Immanuel Church from Benjamin Henry Latrobe and Robert Mills's survey of New Castle, 1804. This shows the church as originally built in 1703. (Courtesy of the Delaware Public Archives.)

## Chapter 2 – Great Expectations, Practical Accomplishments

Evidence indicates that the Anglican church attracted people from various classes and groups. George Keith's SPG letters mention preaching to a diverse audience. In 1704 the Reverend Evan Evans, asking the SPG to send a Welsh-speaking missionary to New Castle because of the number of inhabitants from that region, noted that many parishioners were not well off. Ross's first substantive letter to the SPG explained that few people immediately committed themselves to his ministry because "[m]any hereabout [were] of a long time led away by Dissenting Ministers." Lamentably, Ross's 1728 list of contributions to the church building included only the large givers, though he mentioned that less well-to-do parishioners gave numerous smaller gifts for the building.[14]

The largest supporters of the new church were the same individuals who hoped to further New Castle's economic position. In the 1728 report, the Reverend Ross named forty-four individuals as the major subscribers to the church construction of 1704–1705. Of the twenty-five identifiable New Castle County subscribers, the vast majority were Anglicans living in town. A few were artisans—James Miller was a shipwright and Wessel Alrichs was a goldsmith—and eight subscribers had lived in Delaware before 1682. Alrichs was descended from one of the leading Dutch families in Delaware, and William Tongue's family had come over in the Swedish migration, though by 1708 both actively participated in the Anglican congregation. Nevertheless, the majority of subscribers can best be described as recently arrived, from northern England or Scotland, with a mercantile and landed interest in town. Richard Halliwell, Robert and John French, James and Hercules Coutts, and Samuel Lowman were all major contributors to the new building.[15]

Immanuel Church represented a newly energized force that had insinuated itself into the region—religious competition. The establishment of the Anglican congregation was only one of several indications that churches were vital to the re-formation of the community. The 1700s saw a renaissance in religious activity, especially church-building, in and around New Castle. Those congregations also organized themselves, tied themselves to greater networks of fellow believers, and established their own hierarchical structures, all within this same period. For New Castle this meant the construction of three churches in town and two nearby, all open by 1710. Religious renaissance began before the Anglicans built their church. The Swedes constructed an edifice near what is now Wilmington in 1698 and continued their rather limited ministry to Lutherans. The newly-arrived Welsh Tract Baptists built a wooden church two miles south of present-day Newark, maintaining two aspects of religious life in short supply in the county, a building and a regular supply of pastors. Like the Lutherans they remained on the periphery of New Castle's influence and their doctrine was exclusive rather than inclusive. Unlike the older congregation, however, the Baptists were in a position to attract Britons. The New Castle Anglicans recognized the threat and in 1704 requested a Welsh-speaking pastor to counter it.[16]

The nearly defunct Reformed church in New Castle experienced a metamorphosis at the turn of the century due, as in the Anglican development, to increased local interest and the efforts of nearby Presbyterians. Important to this effort was Francis Mackemie, an itinerant minister who made several trips to New Castle to preach to the old Dutch laity and the Scots and Scotch-Irish newcomers, noting the decrepit condition of the old Dutch church. Perhaps his intervention spurred John Wilson, a New England minister, to move to New Castle in 1698. By 1700 Wilson was pastor of a Presbyterian-style congregation at the old church. He so rejuvenated his parishioners that they joined the Philadelphia presbytery at its inception in 1706. Two years later, the Presbyterians had constructed their own brick church just off the green opposite the Church of England structure. Theirs was a slower process than that of the Anglicans because of fewer provincial and no English resources, although local residents such as William Howston contributed handsomely.[17]

## Chapter 2 – Great Expectations, Practical Accomplishments

The Friends meeting also entered into the competition, though on weakened terms. The congregation experienced less growth from immigrants than other churches; neither did its members resolve the issue of a central meeting place. Indeed, in 1706 the meeting officially split, giving responsibility for the certificates of commendation to two sets of men, four from New Castle itself and four for the area north of Christiana Creek. Soon the two congregations were meeting separately each week but joined together for the monthly meeting.

Nevertheless, the monthly meeting decided to build a meetinghouse in New Castle. In June 1707 the meeting appointed four men—Cornelius Empson, George Robinson, George Harlan, and Thomas Hollingsworth—to confer about erecting a building. Within two months Hollingsworth was in charge of raising a subscription, which process lasted about a year. In May 1708 the meeting appointed men to contract with workers to build a forty-by-twenty foot meetinghouse. Perhaps the New Castle site was a compromise for the dispersed Friends; also, that the Anglicans and Presbyterians had already built their structures gave the Quakers an extra incentive to locate in town.[18]

The religious activity in the first decade of the eighteenth century was not accidental; rather, it demonstrates several things about New Castle society. The level of activity indicates a new impetus in community life. Although the rise in religious activity involved many factors including competition among the various sects and a sense of community-building, it is clear that the New Castle gentry were a major force in developing new community institutions. Their efforts, and those of others in New Castle who competed with them, brought an energy and impetus to the community that had been overshadowed by Philadelphia's meteoric rise.

### CHALLENGING PHILADELPHIA

Despite that revitalized energy in New Castle, the town had already lost in its attempt to vie with Philadelphia for dominance on the Delaware River. Indeed, by 1720 New Castle's own residents were turning elsewhere for port facilities. A hint of New Castle's reduced importance appears as early as 1710 in the sale of front lots. Before 1710 optimism had manifested itself in the sustained interest in the town's front and bank (water) lots. Between 1700 and 1710, eighteen men applied for twenty-two lots; indeed, New Castle appeared to be an alternative port for one Philadelphian, Thomas Tress, who bought a front lot and applied for a water lot in 1708. Between 1710 and 1720, however, only two men bought lots facing the Delaware River in New Castle. Such inactivity might suggest the gentry's dominance of that property, but this was not the case. While land sales in much of the county were strong, interest in New Castle's waterfront property lagged after 1710.[19]

Three other signs point to New Castle's decline as an Atlantic seaport. Shreds of surviving correspondence suggest that the town's merchants were unable to stop Philadelphia's infiltration of Delaware markets. Delaware farmers, especially Quakers, preferred doing business with Philadelphia merchants to dealing with those of New Castle. Already in 1716 Sarah Rodney was sending hides, barley, tobacco, and wheat to Philadelphia merchants in return for European goods. Although New Castle merchants were geographically closer, ties of religion and family encouraged her to deal with the more distant vendors. In addition, proprietary ties ensured connections between New Castle County and Philadelphia. Penn's agents under the direction of James Logan collected taxes, mortgage payments, and quitrents, and when the Delaware residents paid in kind, Philadelphia merchants rather than those in New Castle sold the goods for the proprietary. Even such gentry as John French and George Dakeyne, collecting quitrents for the proprietary, forged business ties in Philadelphia. In such ways did many Delaware farmers turn away from New Castle.[20]

The records of John Williams's carpentry business also testify to the decline of New Castle's Atlantic economy. Williams's

## Chapter 2 – Great Expectations, Practical Accomplishments

accounts prior to 1710 show that he had constructed several coastal vessels and an ocean-going ship for James Coutts. After 1710, however, Williams did no other maritime work; rather he remained busy constructing homes for New Castle residents. Although few records of New Castle shipwrights have survived to corroborate the shift in Williams's patterns of work, Philadelphia's ship registry records do not show any New Castle-built ships after 1715. This business had either moved to Philadelphia or farther south to Appoquinimink by 1710.[21]

Even the primary actors in New Castle's ascendancy seemed to lose interest in their initial vision for New Castle. Between 1705 and 1720 the number of the town's Atlantic traders declined, and those who remained often searched for other, more dependable, sources of income. Several major merchants died, including William Howston in 1707, Hercules Coutts in 1711, Robert French in 1713, and Richard Halliwell in 1719. Hercules's brother James Coutts remained a resident of the town through the end of the decade, but his interest in town affairs declined rapidly. As tobacco prices continued to drop, he and others interested in the trade with Maryland looked for different opportunities. One might speculate that he was often away on ventures; sometime after 1720, he and his business had left town. Similarly Halliwell focused more attention on his Delaware landholdings. Joseph Wood returned to Chester County where he pursued political office and landholding. While other merchants remained in town, they diversified their interests. John French and Jaspar Yeates invested more time in government service, land speculation, and their gristmills on Christiana Creek while keeping their hands in mercantile activities. Although Yeates designated himself a New Castle merchant, his will shows that, at least at the time of his death in 1719, his mercantile holdings were in Chester rather than in New Castle. While several merchants such as Sylvester Garland remained active in town, others abandoned at least a portion of their dream for New Castle.[22]

Few entrepreneurs rushed to New Castle to pick up the pieces. Anthony Howston moved from London to take over his brother's business after 1707; during the next decade William Battell arrived in town, married a daughter of John French, and took over some of his mercantile operations. An examination of the wills of the other gentry, however, demonstrates a paucity of interest in New Castle port among their heirs. Robert French's will gave his bank lot to his son Daniel; at the same time it stipulated that Daniel attend Glasgow University to become a "divine or Phisitian." There is no evidence that Daniel returned to New Castle. In much the same way, Richard Halliwell's will gave his houses, front lots, and bank lots to his brother Thomas, who made no effort to use them. Unlike Baltimore a decade later, New Castle's factors failed to evolve into a class of native-born merchants with contacts in the Caribbean or across the Atlantic, and the town's earlier Atlantic aspirations were seemingly remote to residents by 1720.

### New Castle's New Orientation

New-Castle, the Capital of the County of New-Castle, is a handsome well-built Town, standing upon an Eminence, which gives you a pleasant View from the River Delaware.... There are now above 500 handsome houses and Foundations for several more. As it is daily increasing in Wealth by Trade, we may imagine it will increase in Buildings and Inhabitants, I have been informed they have discovered in the Neighborhood of this Town a fine Iron Mine.

So wrote a visitor to New Castle in the mid-1720s, remarking about the appearance of the town's economic growth. Like this visitor, New Castle's residents were still quite optimistic about the town's prospects. Uncertainty about the county's western border had lessened as the Penn family and Lord Baltimore turned to contest the valuable land on the frontier and in southern Delaware. The Lower

*Chapter 2 – Great Expectations, Practical Accomplishments*

Counties were ruled by a sympathetic lieutenant governor committed to a strong Delaware, perhaps balancing the power of Pennsylvania. Finally, as the visitor had pointed out, several new opportunities promised a brighter economic future for New Castle in place of the chances lost during the previous decade.[23]

New Castle's residents attempted to take advantage of their proximity to the frontier. Instead of competing with Philadelphia as the area's major trading center, they turned to supplying the growing population in New Castle County with such goods and services as barrels and beer, bricks and imports. There is also some evidence of trade with Indians. Artisans and mechanics in town made their livings by providing the neighboring farmers with services; innkeepers continued to lodge travelers between the Middle Colonies and the southern Tidewater. In addition, New Castle continued to serve as the political and governmental center of the county, adding a number of civil servants to its population.

Because of New Castle's new orientation, the issues confronting the town changed. For example, a perennial problem finally had to be addressed because of the limits it was placing on the town. The marshland surrounding town had made the inhabitants susceptible to recurrent sickness. The swamps also limited the physical growth of the town; by 1710 New Castle residents had claimed most of the area bounded within the swamps, and the town could not expand unless the swamps were drained. Efforts to drain the swamps, or at least provide passageways through them, had been ongoing since the early Dutch years, but no one had been able to deal effectively with the problem.

New Castle residents also recognized the importance of expanding passage from the town to the west. Without a river or stream flowing from the west, access to the town was limited by the swampy land that surrounded it on three sides. Since Dutch days a pathway had led from New Castle to the two lower counties. By 1700 the county had established a second road north toward Philadelphia and one west through Christiana over to Elk River in Maryland. The repair of those roads was a constant headache, though entry to the borough depended on their condition. If New Castle's location on the Delaware afforded an avenue to the ocean, it provided less access to the hinterland.[25]

A group of residents attempted to solve that problem by draining the nearby swamps. Led by Jaspar Yeates, certain lot owners petitioned the proprietor for the right to drain the marshes on the south side of town below the common land; they promised to pay the proprietor 20 shillings per acre and provide all labor for the project. The group, comprised almost entirely of townspeople, not only desired to expand the size of the town, but planned to make a profit from their efforts by using that land for their private businesses. But the improvement did not occur in 1715, either because the commissioners of property did not deal with the request or the petitioners found it inconvenient to proceed with their efforts, perhaps because of the tumultuous political climate.[26]

William Keith's accession to the position of lieutenant governor encouraged New Castle residents to proceed with their plans to give the town greater access to the west. When an expanded group of investors reapplied for the right to drain the same swamp in 1717, the commissioners of property finally surveyed the marsh. In just over a year the petitioners had finished the drainage and the commissioners granted them a total of seventeen acres in New Castle.[27]

Their success demonstrates a new-found interest in New Castle land far from the bank lots of a decade before. Moreover, an examination of the petitioners of 1717 indicates a new working relationship with outsiders. John French and Jaspar Yeates petitioned for use of the land, as did one John Land, a relatively wealthy bricklayer and a parishioner at Immanuel Church. The other New Castle petitioner was Presbyterian physician Patrick Reilly. The three other identifiable petitioners were showing a new interest in town; Gilbert Falconer, Isaac Norris, and James Logan were Philadelphia Quakers.

## Chapter 2 – Great Expectations, Practical Accomplishments

Falconer was beginning to speculate in Lower Counties land, sometimes in conjunction with several of the English party. Norris and Logan, two of the most prominent Pennsylvania merchants and allies of the proprietary, showed little concern that they might be strengthening New Castle's competitive position by investing in the town's improvement. Logan's official connection with the proprietary also intimates an attempt by the Penn family to foster ties with the townspeople who had hitherto striven to break the old proprietary bonds.

New Castle's orientation was significant because of the influx of new immigrants, mostly the Scots-Irish, into the Delaware Valley after 1715. Presbyterian Scots-Irish who had been trickling into the Delaware Valley for a decade began to pour into the Delaware River

*Amstel House, no date. Dr. John Finney built this elegant house at the corner of Fourth and Delaware Streets in 1738. It is now a museum of the New Castle Historical Society. (Courtesy of the Historical Society of Delaware.)*

ports of Philadelphia, Lewes, and most particularly New Castle. Long-term problems of rising rents and falling wages combined with such natural disasters as drought and smallpox had forced Protestant Ulster residents to search for new homes, and many looked toward the frontier areas of the New World. New Castle was a favorite debarkation point for these settlers before the migration moved northward toward New York after 1730; it was the first port along the Delaware River with fresh drinking water and with sufficient facilities to unload passengers. A lack of records makes it difficult to gauge the exact number of immigrants, but residents noticed their effect. Already by 1723 a Presbyterian minister counted, "Near to two hundred Families have come into our parts from Ireland, and more are following." In late 1727 James Logan reported, "We have from the North of Ireland great numbers yearly, 8 or 9 ships this last fall discharged at New Castle." Two years later the Pennsylvania Gazette estimated that 4,500 people had come through New Castle in the previous ten years. That figure was probably high; a modern scholar figures the total number of immigrants to the entire Delaware Valley as somewhere between 3,500 and 5,000. While the figure pales in comparison to the immigration waves in the 1740s, 1760s, and 1770s, Delaware's inhabitants felt the change.[28]

The Scots-Irish immigration initially gave New Castle residents opportunities for economic and political growth, offsetting the decade-long decline in its Atlantic trade. Rather than compete with Philadelphia for primacy on the Delaware, New Castle's residents turned to supplying the growing population in New Castle County, which had always been a steady market for the town's goods and services. George Ross described the occupations of his town parishioners as largely artisanal; people worked at "retailing of goods, Rum sugar & Molassos together with some European Goods, some enjoyed posts in the Government and others got their Livings by their handy Crafts as Carpenters smiths and Shoemakers." Their importance to the town shows in their increasing accessibility to the

## Chapter 2 – Great Expectations, Practical Accomplishments

Anglican congregation's lay leadership. By 1718 James Sykes, a feltmaker, was chosen a church warden; two years later the tanner James Merreweather was elected to the vestry.[29]

The new flood of immigrants furnished townspeople with an expanding market. While some of the immigrants remained in the area, buying or renting the remaining open space in New Castle County, most of the Scots-Irish used the town as a provisioning point for their departure to lands farther west. Because so many Scots-Irish landed in New Castle, its provisioners, artisans, and mechanics often had the first opportunity to supply their needs. As "the chief and best Town & most comodiously situated for Trade and Navigation," New Castle residents furnished the newcomers with resources and supplies. The number of New Castle residents who ran inns for the travelers rose dramatically. John Williams's carpentry business changed its focus again after 1720. By this time he completely ceased shipbuilding and also built fewer houses than in the previous decade; instead, he kept busy repairing broken items, and building furniture and caskets.[30]

This newest immigration also forced a greater development of political infrastructure, with New Castle becoming more of a governmental and administrative center. Governor Keith strove to defend land titles by aggressively protecting western borders from Marylanders. An important innovation was the introduction of a land bank to ease the hard money shortage in Delaware. Thus Keith provided both easier access to landholding and a medium of exchange for the Lower Counties, whose residents were receptive to its possibilities. The Loan Office in New Castle kept busy providing mortgages for land and bonds for the local currency.[31]

Immigration encouraged development of county and provincial bureaucracies as well. As early as 1722 the General Court of Quarter Sessions heard a petition regarding the taxing of newcomers. The Assembly also established an Orphans Court that met regularly after 1722, perhaps in response to the problems of younger immigrants overrunning the county. In their 1726–7 session the Lower Counties Assembly, meeting in New Castle, passed a law requiring vessels with sick passengers to moor at least one mile offshore until the captain procured a landing permit signed by either the governor or two justices. The community also upgraded its jail and the county courthouse, where the Delaware Assembly met. In 1732, after William Kelsey burnt down the jail and adjoining courthouse in an attempt to escape, the authorities determined to erect a new courthouse, which served as the colonial capitol building until the Revolutionary War.[32]

The growing bureaucratization of New Castle attracted new professionals to town, though not in large numbers. Because of the government and legal work, a few lawyers such as Andrew Hamilton, David French, and William Shaw were beginning to practice in New Castle County. French—probably a nephew of John French—and Shaw chose to live in New Castle; both became involved in provincial government. Although the town could not generate enough publishing to support a printer, the county kept busy two full-time scriveners, Robert Robertson and John Legate, who lived in town.[33]

Thus, it appeared as if New Castle's position was not necessarily weakened by the shift in its orientation toward the frontier. The gentry could keep their plans for the town alive if they could turn their interests westward. They could retain control of the backcountry through their political leverage. A steady influx of immigrants would provide economic leverage to the town and cement their roles as Delaware's leading citizens. While the source of its power might change, New Castle might still retain its hold on northern Delaware.

## New Castle and Wilmington

In 1752, George Ross wrote to the SPG about the trials and tribulations of serving a congregation in "the mean village of New Castle." Two years earlier he had attributed many of the town's woes to Wilmington, "an upstart village" which had quickly overtaken

*Chapter 2 – Great Expectations, Practical Accomplishments*

New Castle as the chief settlement in Delaware. For Ross, who had involved himself in the earlier attempts to make New Castle a formidable force on the Delaware River, this inversion of roles was particularly galling.[34]

From the comments of Ross and others one senses an erosion of spirit, a deterioration of optimism as New Castle lost ground to the new community of Wilmington between 1735 and 1755. Such firmly-rooted institutions as the Presbyterian and Quaker meetings were shaken, and Ross even questioned the strength of his own congregation. During this period the region was developing what James Henretta has described as a proto-capitalistic economy. While Philadelphia dominated the export economy and Wilmington residents discovered opportunities to exploit the nearby rivers and the wheat-growing region both in Delaware and in Lancaster County, New Castle was shut out of such enterprises. The townspeople, accepting New Castle's secondary position, fell back on other means by which to make a living. Such diverse enterprises as weaving, brewing, inn-keeping, and government services, while not as grand as the export trade the earlier gentry had envisioned for the town, provided a way of life for the now reduced expectations of the townspeople.[35]

Wilmington's successes stirred New Castle residents to competition in a modest way. Wilmington's market, granted by its 1739 charter, encouraged New Castle retailers to ask permission for their own market, to which the Lower Counties Assembly had agreed by 1740. Wilmington's challenge awakened several local entrepreneurs to redevelop their market. Almost a decade later Ezekiel Sykes reported that New Castle also held a semiannual fair, in competition with the fairs of Wilmington, Chester, and Philadelphia.[36]

Nevertheless, there is little doubt that after 1735 New Castle experienced a period of economic depression. Robert Hempstead, of New London, Pennsylvania, upon visiting New Castle in 1749, described the town.

> Here is a fine courthouse and church and many good buildings but some that were large and handsome are much decayed and falling down... there was no wharf but what is dry at low water around it.

He noticed both the declining population of the town and one of the reasons for that decline, a loss of port facilities. New Castle had long since lost its ship-building services. While local shipping still abounded in New Castle County, especially along Appoquinimink and Duck creeks to the south and on the Christiana River to the north, hopes for a town that prospered from the Atlantic economy were long gone.[37]

George Ross's semiannual parish reports indicated several trends in the community. Required to send the information to the SPG in London twice a year, Ross provided quantified reports after 1740. In 1741 he reported the number of inhabitants in New Castle as 830. Two years later he reported that 900 people lived in his parish, which he probably saw as extending into New Castle Hundred; during the next ten years that number declined until 1752 when he reported a total of 800 residents. While Wilmington's population was increasing, New Castle's had, at best, stabilized.[38]

Ross's comments indicated other changes in New Castle's population. Already in 1736 Ross reported that the people attending Immanuel "are generally poor & of a mean appearance... who sit now in the Pews formerly Posses't by those who were Reputed Gentlemen." Five years later he noted that the town's "trade and Number of Inhabitants" had decreased substantially enough to affect his congregation. Calling New Castle a village in 1745, Ross described conditions as ruinous, where even "the Meeting House is wholly deserted." In 1745 he explained that the town's population consisted of farmers, artisans, and "& Such as work for daily Wages" rather than the great merchants of earlier decades.

> [F]ormerly we could vie with our neighbours in Colls [Colonels], Captains & Publick Officers. Our desolation

*Chapter 2 – Great Expectations, Practical Accomplishments*

is so great we have several fair houses without Inhabitants, a Port without Trade & consequently an useless Collector.[39]

Ross's mood towards the town changed very little in his last several pieces of correspondence with the Society. In 1750 he blamed the town's problems on Wilmington, "an upstart village lying on a Neighboring creek, which yields a convenient port to the adjacent County." Two years later he described his ministry in "the mean village of New Castle Where little or nothing occurring beside the common offices of a Settled Cure." Perhaps advancing age and declining health obscured his perspective about his town, but Ross obviously expected New Castle's prospects to change very little in the near future.[40]

One aspect of the New Castle community that changed very little was its diversity, as Ross noted in his comments to the SPG. His reports divided the population of his parish—New Castle and its nearby environs—into Anglicans and dissenters, specifically citing in addition the numbers of Quakers and "Papists." Ross consistently enumerated the dissenters, in which he included both Presbyterians and Baptists, as the largest population in his parish. The average population of dissenters over that ten-year period was 560, while the number of Anglicans averaged 261, or less than one-half of the number of dissenters. Quakers in and around town were so few that he did not even count them after the first reports in 1741.

In contrast, a number of Roman Catholics showed up in New Castle during this time. While there had always been one or two Catholics in town since the 1670s because New Castle's port attracted sailors of various nationalities, their presence was more visible after 1740, at least to Ross. The Venerable Society had specifically urged its missionaries to be aware of Papists in their parishes, and Ross kept close count of them. His 1741 report counted twenty-eight Catholics, and the subsequent numbers fluctuated anywhere between fifteen in 1747 and fifty as early as 1743 and in his last report in 1752, for a ten-year average of thirty-seven. In 1743 he commented that the local Catholics were common laborers. They might have come from three directions: some were Marylanders working their way east; several were probably itinerant sailors who had stopped in town for a time; and a few might have been immigrants who had joined the Scots-Irish migration across the ocean. Nevertheless, their presence added to an already diverse population.[41]

The continuing diversity of its population, on top of the town's loss of economic and political power, may have slowed the development of community institutions in town. While Wilmington and other New Castle County communities were establishing schools, New Castle's residents put off formal instruction of their young until the revolutionary era. Unlike inhabitants of the younger Delaware town, New Castle citizens of the later period showed no interest in joining Philadelphia's Library Society or Franklin's Junto. Despite the need for government-sponsored printing in town, there was no talk of a newspaper; New Castle residents, like their northern counterparts, used the *Pennsylvania Gazette* to post notices of interest to the region. There is evidence that lawyers congregating in town for legal or governmental purposes functioned as an informal "fraternity" but there were few other signs of voluntary community organization.

Even the bedrock of the community—the churches—reflect the town's fortunes. The Friends meetinghouse in New Castle suffered from neglect and underuse. In 1750, the New Castle Friends was downgraded in status to a Preparative Meeting within the Wilmington Monthly Meeting, but eight years later the New Castle meeting was completely laid down. While the New Castle Presbyterian congregation did not collapse, support for the town's church suffered. A 1750 list of the pew rents shows 27 people paying for that privilege. As George Ross counted approximately 485 dissenters in the New Castle area in 1750, this represents a very weak support for the congregation. The inability to keep a pastor for any length of time and the tumults of the Great Awakening, as well as the town's fortunes, kept the congregation divided.[42]

*Chapter 2 – Great Expectations, Practical Accomplishments*

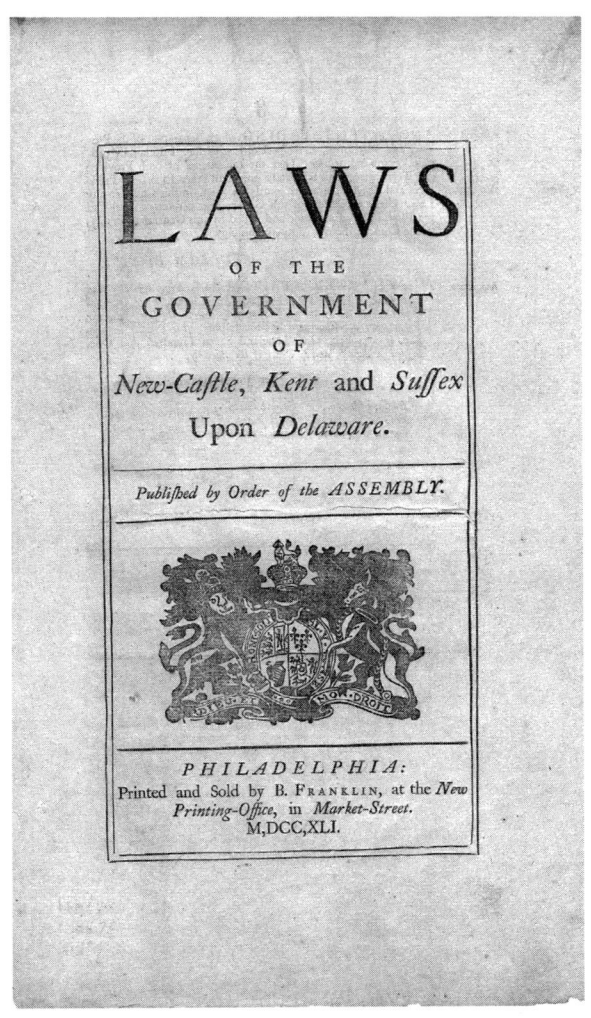

Laws of the Government of New Castle, Kent and Sussex Upon Delaware
*(Philadelphia: B. Franklin, 1741). Delaware's colonial Assembly met at New
Castle, but since there were no printers in Delaware until the early 1760s,
official documents were printed in Philadelphia. Benjamin Franklin served as
Delaware's official printer from 1729 until 1760.
(Courtesy of the Historical Society of Delaware.)*

Yet the future was not completely bleak, for some New Castle townspeople found ways to take advantage of opportunities in the region. The town had retained several important functions from the early part of the century, including serving as a point of entry. While the bulk of the Scots-Irish immigration had shifted either to New York or the Chesapeake, New Castle attracted some continuing, and perhaps somewhat illicit, immigration. The *Pennsylvania Gazette* reported on December 17, 1742, that a ship from Londonderry, Ireland, bound for New Castle ran aground with the loss of many lives. New Castle may also have been the shipping point for flaxseed for the Irish linen industry. In 1746 and 1747 the *Gazette* reported that several ships from northern Ireland had experienced trouble with French and Spanish privateers before they arrived in New Castle. The town also continued to serve as the county seat and colonial capital, attracting people involved in legal, political, and provincial affairs, both for the long term and for short stays. New Castle remained a transfer point between the Middle Colonies and the South, as evidenced by the continuing proliferation of taverns and inns. Slator Clay, for example, an up-and-coming yeoman, announced in 1741 the opening of his public house in New Castle to attract the attention of travelers. Residents found ways to adapt to new conditions.

The actions of the early-eighteenth-century New Castle residents in great part shaped the subsequent development of the community. Their interest in such community institutions as churches manifests itself today in the continuation of Immanuel Church and the New Castle Presbyterian Church. Their attempts to improve the town's physical condition by developing its port facilities and controlling the surrounding marshland provided the next generations with useful infrastructure. Their efforts to expand the town's economic interests across the Atlantic and toward the frontier, while failing to provide their own generation with economic security, established useful limits for future residents. Their recognition and accept-

## Chapter 2 – Great Expectations, Practical Accomplishments

ance of the diverse ethnic and religious population in and around town set a precedent for toleration in the colonies. Their longstanding efforts in promoting Lower Counties interests against Pennsylvania, the Penn proprietary, Maryland, and even royal incursions manifested an independent nature for the colony, and later state, of Delaware.

---

[1] Wayne Andrews, "A Glance at New York in 1697: The Travel Directory of Dr. Benjamin Bullivant," *The New-York Historical Society Quarterly* 40 (Jan. 1956): 136. This article is taken from sections of the author's dissertation, "Anglicization in a 'Frenchified, Scotchified, Dutchified Place': New Castle, Delaware, 1690–1750" (Ph.D. diss., New York University, 1994). The author would like to thank Jeff Walz and Constance Cooper for providing useful comments on drafts of this article.

[2] The preceding description of New Castle in 1700 has been compiled from several sources including New Castle County Warrants and Surveys, various descriptions of the town, and research done by Louise B. Heite in "New Castle under the Duke of York: A Stable Community," (M.A. thesis, University of Delaware, 1978). See also C.A. Weslager, "Watermills, Windmills, Horsemills—and a Tidemill: Early Colonial Grain Mills in Delaware," *Delaware History* 14 ( 1970): 52–61 (hereafter cited as *DH*).

[3] For the 1693 and 1697 assessments, see Proprietary Notes Re: Lower Counties (Sussex County Court Record), Penn MSS, Reference Reel R-76 (unnumbered pages), Delaware Public Archives, Dover, Delaware (hereafter DPA). For the individuals listed, see *Records of the Court of New Castle on the Delaware 1676–1681* (Lancaster, Penn., 1904), 2: 46 (hereafter cited as *NC Records*).

[4] David G. Hackett, *The Rude Hand of Innovation: Religion and Social Order in Albany, New York, 1652–1836* (New York, 1991), pp. 23–26.

[5] Craig W. Horle and Marianne S. Wokeck, *Lawmaking and Legislators in Pennsylvania: A Biographical Dictionary*, vol. 1 (Philadelphia, 1991 ) is a good place to start tracing the lives of these New Castle leaders.

[6] See the bribery example in Robert Quary to Francis Nicholson, Philadelphia, July 9, 1698, *Calendar of State Papers, Colonial Series, America and West Indies*, vol. 16 (London: Her Majesty's Stationary Office, 1860–1933; reprint Kraus Reprint, 1964), pp. 396–98, #760v (hereafter cited as CSPC); Penn to Council of Trade and Plantations, no date, CSPC, 20: p. 407, #638; Randolph to Council of Trade and Plantations, Nov. 5, 1700, CSPC, 18: p. 634, #906;

Quary to Council of Trade and Plantations, March 6, 1700/1, CSPC, 18: p. 107, #190.

[7] Quary to Nicholson, July 9, 1698, CSPC, 16: pp. 396–98, #760v; Quary to Council of Trade and Plantations, Dec. 7, 1702, CSPC, 21: pp. 14–15, #16; "Address of the Representatives of the Three Lower Counties to the Council of Trade and Plantations," Philadelphia, Oct. 25, 1701, CSPC, 20: pp. 182–83, #270.

[8] The lot information was taken from New Castle County Warrants & Surveys in DPA (hereafter cited as NCC Warrants). For Claypoole's conversion, see "Mr. Keith's Narrative," Sept. 15, 1704, SPG Journals, Appendix B, #50.

[9] Early interest in the New Castle dikes can be found, among other places, in a 1676 order to the county sheriff, Nov. 11, 1676, *NC Records*, p. 25. For the later involvement of French and Halliwell, see NCC Warrants, 1–28–1701Q, D3-58 #850.

[10] James Logan to William Howston, 2–12–1703Q, Logan Papers, James Logan Letterbooks, vol. 2, p. 22, Historical Society of Pennsylvania, Philadelphia. See also Richard Rodney, Newlin Booth, and Donald Banks, eds., *New Castle Common* (Wilmington, 1944), pp. 6–7.

[11] Jenkins to Secretary, Aug. 26, 1708, Society for the Propagation of the Gospel in Foreign Parts, Letterbooks, Series A, vol. 4, #LXIII (hereafter cited as SPG MSS A). For the economic activities of Yeates, see Penn to Council of Trade and Plantations, no date, CSPC, 20: p. 407, #638. The Private Accounts of John Williams, Cabinetmaker & Joiner 1700–1757, RG#9025, NCC Private Accounts, DPA; Penn to John Evans, 3–15–1701Q, *Papers of William Penn*, vol. 4, p. 576 (hereafter cited as *PWP*).

[12] Christopher M. Agnew, ed., *God with Us: A Continuing Presence and the Vital Records Taken from the Parish Registers of Immanuel Church, New Castle, Delaware* (privately printed, 1986), p. 7. According to "Mr. Keith's Narrative," he preached in New Castle three times in 1703 and 1704. "Journal of Rev. John Sharpe," *Pennsylvania Magazine of History and Biography* 40 (1916): 287 (hereafter cited as *PMHB*). Nelson Waite Rightmyer, *The Anglican Church in Delaware* (Philadelphia, 1947), pp. 6–8, mentions early worship sites.

[13] Daniel Roberts, "Historical Architecture of Immanuel Church, New Castle, Delaware," *Pennsylvania Archaeologist* 57 (1987): 1–33. See also Donald Friary, "The Architecture of the Anglican Church in the Northern American Colonies: A Study of Religious, Social, and Cultural Expression" (Ph.D. diss., University of Pennsylvania, 1971), pp. 888–91; and Del Upton, *Holy Things and Profane: Anglican Churches in Colonial Virginia* (New York, 1986).

[14] "Mr. Keith's Narrative;" Rev. Evan Evans, "A Sumary Account of the State of the Church in the Province of Pennsylvania," SPG Journals, Appendix B #56; Ross to Secretary, May 17, 1706, SPG MSS A, 2: #CLXVIII; Ross to

## Chapter 2 – Great Expectations, Practical Accomplishments

Secretary, March 1, 1727/8, SPG MSS A, 20: 116–23.

[15] Ross to Secretary, March 1, 1727/8; Thomas Holcomb, *Sketch of the Early Ecclesiastical Affairs in New Castle, Delaware, and History of Immanuel Church* (Wilmington, 1890), p. 42.

[16] For the Lutherans, see Henry C. Conrad, *Old Swedes Church, Wilmington, Delaware* (Wilmington, 1899), pp. 5–9. For the Baptist meeting house, see Morgan Edwards, "Materials Towards a History of the Baptists in Delaware State," *PMHB* 3 (1885): 46–49. See also Jon Butler, "Power, Authority, and the Origins of American Denominational Order: The English Churches in the Delaware Valley 1680–1730," *Transactions of the American Philosophical Society* 68 (Feb. 1978), part 2, for a worthwhile description of the changes occurring in this region.

[17] For New Castle Presbyterians, a good place to start is J.B. Spotswood, *An Historical Sketch of the Presbyterian Church in New Castle, Delaware* (Philadelphia, 1859).

[18] 6-1690Q, 8-1703Q, 10-1706Q, 3-1707Q, 2-1708Q Kennett Monthly Meeting Minutes on microfilm at Friends Historical Library, Swarthmore College. For Quakers in the Delaware Valley, see Butler, "Power," chap 3.

[19] Simeon Crowther, "The Shipbuilding Industry and Economic Development of the Delaware Valley, 1681–1776" (Ph.D. diss., University of Pennsylvania, 1970); NCC Warrants, especially Thomas Tress, Aug. 3, 1708, T1-18; the two lots after 1710 were a survey for the heirs of Robert Dyer, March 14, 1716/7, D3-45, and a survey for John French, June 8, 1716, F2-51.

[20] For an example of the networking among Friends, see Penn to Evans, 3-15-1707Q, *PWP,* 4: 575–76. Sarah Rodney's experience can be found in Rodney Papers, Historical Society of Delaware, Wilmington. For an example of the reach of Philadelphia merchants, see Dakeyne to Logan, March 14, 1716, Logan Letters.

[21] Williams Accounts. "Ships and Registers for the Port of Philadelphia, 1726–1775," *PMHB* 23 (1899): 260, shows no ships registered were built in New Castle at that time.

[22] Much of the information in this paragraph and the following one can be found in various wills in NCC Wills & Probates, DPA. For the comparison with Baltimore, see Charles G. Steffen, "The Rise of the Independent Merchant in the Chesapeake: Baltimore County, 1660–1769," *Journal of American History* 76 (June 1989): 9–33.

[23] Quotation from [William Rufus Chetwood or Benjamin Victor], The Voyages and Adventures of Captain Robert Boyle in Several Parts of the World, To which is Added the Voyage, Shipwreck, and Miraculous Preservation of Richard Castelman, Gent., (London, 1726), in Harold B.

Hancock, ed., "Descriptions and Travel Accounts of Delaware, 1700–1740," *DH* 10 (Oct. 1962): 125.

[24] On Aug. 16, 1720, the Court of Quarter Sessions issued twelve licenses for operating inns in and around New Castle. Andrew Hesselius reported that an unnamed New Castle merchant pursued a lively trade with Indians; see Amandus Johnson, ed., "The Journals of Andrew Hesselius 1711–1724," *DH* 2 (Sept. 1947): 102.

[25] James T. Lemon, "Urbanization and the Development of Eighteenth-Century Southeastern Pennsylvania and Adjacent Delaware," *William and Mary Quarterly* 24 (Oct. 1967): 528, believes that New Castle never exceeded a population of 600, which it had reached by 1681; he argues that its population was stable between 1700 and 1720. For a description of the road system, see Mark Schaffer, et al, *Final Phase III Investigations of the Whitten Road Site 7NC-D-100, Whitten or Walther Road, County Road 346, New Castle County, Delaware* (Delaware Department of Transportation, Archaeological Series No. 68), pp. 18–19.

[26] Dakeyne to Logan, May 28, 1714, Penn MSS, Additional Misc. Letters, vol. 1, #19, indicates interest before 1715. Warrant to survey New Castle marsh, June 18, 1715, NCC Warrants, Y1-2, #250.

[27] Warrant to Falconer, et al. for 17 acres, 5-20- 1718Q, New Castle County Recorder of Deeds, Penn's Warrants 1682–1694, #322 (RG #2555, Reel #1072), DPA.

[28] Letter of George Gillespie to Rev. John Stirling, in Charles A. Briggs, *American Presbyterianism: Its Origin and Early History* (New York, 1885), p. lxxxiv; Logan to Hannah Penn, fall 1727, in Guy Klett, *Presbyterians in Colonial Pennsylvania* (Philadelphia, 1937), p. 32; *Pennsylvania Gazette*, Jan. 6, 1729/30. For modern estimates about the number of immigrants, see James G. Leyburn, *The Scotch-Irish: A Social History* (Chapel Hill, 1962), p. 180, and Klett, *Presbyterians,* pp. 20, 31-32.

[29] Quote from Ross to Secretary, March 1, 1727/8, p. 162. April 14, 1718, and April 18, 1720, vestry minutes, Minutebook, Immanuel Church, New Castle, Delaware (in possession of Immanuel Church), pp. 14, 17.

[30] Quote from Ross to Secretary, March 1, 1727/8, p. 159. New Castle County Probate Records show a rising number of innkeepers: Thomas Thompson, 1738–48; Abraham Flemming, 1724; Baldwin Johnson, 1721; Jeremiah Shennon, 1726-9; DPA. Williams Accounts.

[31] Thomas H. Wendel, "The Life and Writings of Sir William Keith, Lieutenant-Governor of Pennsylvania and the Three Lower Counties 1717–1726" (Ph.D. diss., University of Washington, 1964),pp.153–54.

## Chapter 2 – Great Expectations, Practical Accomplishments

[32] General Court of Quarter Sessions, Feb. 20, 1721/2, in New Castle County General Court of Quarter Sessions Pleas Docket Book, p. 320, Record Group #2805; DPA; New Castle, folder 1, Box 82C, HSD Manuscript Files, Wilmington; Alice Guerant, "Old New Castle Courthouse: Test Excavations in the Sheriff's Yard and Alley" (Dover: Bureau of Archaeology and Historical Preservation, Aug. 29, 1984). For information about the Kelsey incident, see *Pennsylvania Gazette,* March 13, 1729/30.

[33] The three lawyers are mentioned in the two extant docket books of GQ Sessions, 1717–9 and 1727–9, DPA. For the clerks, see New Castle County Probate Records of Thomas Gozell, 1732, and John Legate, 1744, DPA.

[34] Quotes are from Ross to Secretary, March 27, 1750, SPG MSS B 18: #154 and Sept. 30, 1752, SPG.

[35] James Henretta, "The War for Independence and American Economic Development," in *The Origins of American Capitalism: Collected Essays* (Boston, 1991), pp. 211–14.

[36] Oct. 29, 1740, *Minutes of the House of Assembly of the Three Counties Upon Delaware at Sessions Held at New Castle in the Years 1740–1742* (Dover, 1929), p. 29. The reference to Sykes is in William T. Read, *Life and Correspondence of George Read* (Philadelphia, 1870), p. 316.

[37] The quote is found in George H. Gibson, ed., *The Collected Essays of Richard S. Rodney on Early Delaware* (Wilmington, 1976), p. 183. "Ships Registers," 260, ff. shows few ships registered out of New Castle and the Williams Account shows no shipbuilding activity in the 1730s.

[38] Ross's reports can be found in SPG MSS B, Aug. 4, 1741, 9: #92; March 4, 1742/3, 10: #118; March 6, 1744/5, 12: #44; Sept. 30, 1747, 14: p. 151; and March 26, 1752, 20: #127.

[39] Ross to Secretary, June 15, 1736, SPG MSS A, 25: pp. 329–30; March 4, 1741/2, SPG MSS B, 10: #116; Nov. 23 1745, SPG MSS B, 12: #43.

[40] Ross to Secretary, March 27, 1750, SPG MSS B, 17: #154; Sept. 30, 1752, SPG MSS B, 20: #128.

[41] See Ross's reports, as listed in endnote 38. The first Roman Catholic church in New Castle County was built at Appoquinimink in 1750; see Frederick L. Weis, *The Colonial Churches and the Colonial Clergy of the Middle and Southern States 1607–1776* (Lancaster, Mass., 1938), p. 21.

[42] For the Quaker meeting, see Herbert Standing, "Quakers in Delaware in the Time of William Penn," *DH* 20 (Winter 1982): 123–47. For the travails of the Presbyterian congregation, see New Castle, Delaware Presbyterian Church, Congregation [Petitions to New Castle Presbytery for a minister 1746–1752], and Trustees [Pew Rents, 1750], in Presbyterian Historical

Society, Philadelphia. Ross to Secretary, Sept. 29, 1750, SPG MSS B, 18: #155.

[43] *Pennsylvania Gazette,* Dec. 17, 1741, Sept. 18, Oct. 9, 1746, and Jan. 6, 1747.

## Voices and Viewpoints

*In the late eighteenth and early nineteenth centuries, the new nation called the United States fascinated everyone. Americans produced geographies and gazetteers describing cities, towns, roads, natural resources, and agricultural products, while foreign visitors published their impressions of their travels. Here are two views of New Castle from such sources. The Duke de la Rochefoucault Liancourt, a Frenchman, visited in the mid 1790s. The American Joseph Scott published his geography of Maryland and Delaware in 1807. Both commented on New Castle's role as a transportation hub, a vital part of the town's economy in the period.*

## Early Travelers' Impressions

*From Duke de la Rochefoucault Liancourt,*
Travels through the United States of North America, *1795*

Newcastle is composed of seventy houses, some of which are of brick, and are built adjacent to each other: the wide streets and the grass plots give it the appearance of an English village. Being the county town, it contains the sessions-house and the prison. The town is built on the Delaware; it does not, however, carry on any direct foreign trade, but confines itself to the coasting trade with Philadelphia.

Newcastle… is the oldest city of this state.

A fund having been raised by way of lottery, sanctioned by the state, for the purpose of building quays at Newcastle, that place now affords shelter to vessels in the winter, and begins to rise from the state of decay into which it had sunk.

Oak is sold at Newcastle for five dollars a cord, and hiccory for nearly seven dollars.... The frequent communication between Philadelphia and Baltimore, and the great traffic between the two cities, have occasioned the establishment of a more speedy means of conveyance of goods and passengers, than by the ordinary land and water carriage.

Four small sloops constantly sail to and from Newcastle and Philadelphia. Regular stages convey the passengers to French-Town, on the Elk-River, about twelve miles distant from Newcastle. Goods are carried there in carts. Other sloops sail down the Elk-River, which empties itself into the Chesapeak, eighteen miles from French-Town, from whence they proceed to Baltimore. The expence of the passage from Philadelphia to Newcastle is three quarters of a dollar, three quarters of a dollar by the stage to French-Town, and one dollar and a quarter from French-Town to Baltimore. This route is impassable during the three or four winter months, at which time the river Delaware is generally frozen.

Newcastle is the true point from which all the Philadelphian ship take their departure. When they are laden, they drop down thither with their pilot, and take in their poultry and vegetables, where the captains who remain at Philadelphia to settle their accounts at the custom-house join them by land, and from whence they sail with the first fair wind.[1]

*From Joseph Scott,* A Geographical Description of the States of Maryland and Delaware, *1807*

*Newcastle,* a post town, and the seat of justice for the county. It is pleasantly situated on the west side of Delaware river, 40 miles below Philadelphia. It contains about 160 houses, and 1200 inhabitants. A great many of the houses have been built within these few years, and some of them in a handsome style. The public buildings are a court house, jail, three public offices, a market house, an academy, in which three schools are kept, a church for Presbyterians, one for Episcopalians, one for Quakers, and one for Roman Catholics. Four public piers are erected in the Delaware, in front of the town, for the protection of shipping in the winter season, and for the better securing the harbor....

[Newcastle] was formerly the seat of government for the three lower counties. Very little business was done in it for a great many years. Its trade began to revive about 15 years ago, since which it has increased considerably. Almost all the vessels bound from Philadelphia to foreign ports, stop here and supply themselves with live stock. A great line of packets and stages passes through it from Philadelphia to Baltimore, by way of Frenchtown. Vast quantities of merchandise are sent by this route, from Philadelphia to the western country. It is at present, one of the greatest thoroughfares for travelling in the United States. There are seven large and well accommodated packets, which sail constantly between this port and Philadelphia, and from 10 to 15 heavy waggons, for the transportation of goods and passengers across the peninsula to Frenchtown; besides four land stages.[2]

[1] Duke de la Rochefoucault Liancourt, *Travels through the United States of North America, ... in the years 1795, 1796, and 1797,* 4 vols. (London, 1800), 3: 536–39

[2] Joseph Scott, *A Geographical Description of the States of Maryland and Delaware* (Philadelphia, 1807), pp. 176–78.

# Chapter Three

In the late 1700s and early 1800s, New Castle actively sought to grow into a small city by developing as a port, transportation center, and county seat. This article is based on the author's dissertation, "A Town Among Cities: New Castle, Delaware, 1780–1840" (Ph.D. dissertation, University of Delaware, 1983).

# A Town Among Cities: New Castle, 1780–1840

*Constance J. Cooper*

Between 1780 and 1840, New Castle based its hopes for success on two apparently permanent features, the Delaware River and the New Castle County courthouse. The 1790s and the opening years of the nineteenth century offered prospects for success, but in time New Castle learned its limitations. Assets that nature and the past had provided could be threatened and even taken away, and resources adequate for a preindustrial commercial town would not be sufficient for success in the urbanizing and industrializing Philadelphia region.

New Castle fought for prosperity and status from a position in the middle of a relatively stable regional urban network. Philadelphia was at the top; although it lost its position as the nation's premier city to New York by 1810, it remained first in the region. As the nation's economy changed in the early nineteenth century, Philadelphia declined as a port and began to develop into a manufacturing center.

Wilmington, Delaware's largest city, came next. Like Philadelphia, its port declined, but, unlike its northern neighbor, Wilmington did not industrialize heavily until after 1840. Also, both the Chesapeake and Delaware Canal and the New Castle and Frenchtown Railroad bypassed it.[1] Although Wilmington certainly grew in the early nineteenth century, it felt trapped; it resented Philadelphia but could not do much about it, and continually scrapped with New Castle.

After New Castle, Newport, Christiana Bridge, and Stanton occupied the lower rungs of the urban ladder. The first two were grain-shipping ports on the Christina River, while Stanton, on a neck between two creeks, developed into a local manufacturing center in the early 1800s.[2] While these towns prospered in the early nineteenth century, they lacked New Castle's drive. They reacted to their neighbor's ambition with petty jealousy and anger rather than outright competition; when New Castle began promoting a turnpike to Frenchtown, the other towns talked of moving the county seat in retaliation.[3] Although New Castle did not compete with these towns, each filled economic roles that New Castle did not. In developing their own advantages, they limited New Castle's possibilities. After around 1830, as the region's transportation and industry changed, Christiana Bridge, Stanton, and Newport faded into quiet villages. By 1840, the regional urban hierarchy was essentially as it had been in the late 1700s, but each city, town, and village was more firmly locked into its place.

## Awakening, 1780–1808

The Revolutionary War and subsequent depression killed New Castle's fragile economic and civic vigor of the 1760s and early 1770s, leaving the town depressed and unpromising. A visitor saw New Castle in the early 1780s as "a little insignificant town" with few "seemly buildings." The town had "no trade" and "the inhabitants seem[ed] not to be active." He suggested that Philadelphia's proximity prevented New Castle from prospering. In contrast, Wilmington

## Chapter 3 – A Town Among Cities

was "a vastly better place, large and busy," with vigorous commerce, a good market, and many new houses under construction.[4] By 1787, conditions had not improved; as one man wrote, "I apprehend Nothing will be saved by keeping the Houses & Lots in New Castle for a Market, as I imagine their value will rather decrease than otherwise."[5]

Even during those bleak years, New Castle's people hoped to move forward, for in 1786 they submitted two requests to the Delaware General Assembly. One was for official town government to replace extralegal town meetings of the war years. New Castle apparently suffered the social consequences of unemployment and poverty, for the citizens hoped to "Discourage Immorality, and to promote the Order, Sobriety, and Interest of said Town."[6] The legislature did not grant this petition. The second request, supported by others in the county as well, was to designate New Castle and Wilmington as free ports with advantageous conditions for trade. The petitions cited New Castle's assets: a pleasant, healthy location, an extensive backcountry, and a deep harbor navigable almost all year. In addition, New Castle had raised money to place protective piers in the harbor. The hope of attracting more trade to Delaware and freeing the state from dependence on Pennsylvania motivated the request for free-port status. The request became law but soon was superseded by the new national constitution.[7]

The depression began to lift after 1789. Wars between France and England from 1793 to 1807 disrupted normal trade and shipping patterns, providing a golden opportunity for the American economy.[8] In New Castle, vigor, growth, and optimism replaced gloom and poverty. The population grew from 823 in 1800 to 1,021 in 1810, an increase of 24 percent. Outsiders commented favorably on the town's appearance and activity, and real estate advertisements described its prospects in glowing terms. Under favorable economic conditions, New Castle recaptured its thwarted civic identity and aspiration and turned some of its deferred dreams into reality.

Two governmental bodies, which townspeople had been seeking to create for a number of years, finally came into being. The Trustees of the Common, guardians of a 1,068-acre tract of common land west of town, received title to the land from the Penn family in 1791 and a state charter in 1792. This allowed them to implement their plan of leasing the land as farms and using the proceeds to benefit the town. In 1797, a state law authorized the creation of town government with taxing authority, in the form of five elected commissioners. Through the years, the Trustees of the Common and the town commissioners worked together to administer and improve the town of New Castle.[9]

The harbor was the major economic focus. With few exceptions, ships stopping in 1797 or before came from Irish ports laden with hundreds of immigrants. Some of the other vessels were in the American coastal trade, while one came from Jamaica.[10] Between 1801 and 1805, the harbor was busier and the ships traveled a wider variety of routes. Although West Indian ports dominated, a few ships came from Europe or Ireland.[11]

Viewing the harbor as the source of prosperity, citizens worked to improve its facilities. The long-awaited piers, structures placed in the water at the harbor's edge to provide protection from ice and storms, were erected in the mid-1790s. A law of 1802 authorized the appointment of a harbormaster, suggesting either that the harbor was busy enough to need supervision, or that New Castle aspired to such a level of activity and in the meantime wanted a symbol of that status. Finally, townspeople petitioned Congress, unsuccessfully, to be made a port of entry, although they did succeed in having the piers placed under federal control and funding. Much of the drive for harbor improvement had the moral, but probably not the financial, support of Philadelphia merchants who saw New Castle as a non-competing auxiliary to their own harbor.[12]

New Castle's primary function in the web of commerce was not buying and selling goods but servicing ships. As the last safe harbor

## Chapter 3 – A Town Among Cities

before putting out to sea and the northernmost port on the Delaware River to stay relatively free of ice in the winter, New Castle was a refuge, especially for ships bound to and from Philadelphia. The town's mercantile specialty was providing supplies for outbound ships. Nearly every contemporary observer commented on it, while saying nothing about New Castle as a general commercial center.[13]

In the end, however, the harbor's prospects were limited. When applying in 1789 to become the state's first federal customs collector, James Booth presented his hometown as favorably as possible, but still had to admit that almost all of Delaware's foreign trade originated in Wilmington.[14] New Castle was neither an owner nor a builder of ships, nor was it a major commercial center. In the late eighteenth century, New Castle owned two vessels in foreign trade and five in coastal shipping, compared with Wilmington's fifteen ships in foreign trade and seventeen coasting vessels.[15] New Castle was primarily a refuge and a supply center. Vessels often stopped there, but the real business was done elsewhere.

New Castle's riverfront location also made it a vital link in the regional and national transportation network. The Delmarva Peninsula was a major obstacle to travel between Philadelphia and Baltimore. All-land or all-water routes were expensive and inconvenient; the bearable compromise at this time was a combination. Travelers went by boat from Philadelphia to some point on the Delaware side of the peninsula, by land across to Chesapeake Bay, and again by water to Baltimore. Development of the route was an important part of New Castle's thwarted pre-Revolutionary spurt; when travel and trade revived in the 1790s, so did this route.

A visiting Frenchman described his 1794 journey from Baltimore to Philadelphia in detail. His boat left Baltimore at eight-thirty one morning. It reached Frenchtown, New Castle's western counterpart, at one o'clock the next morning, but the passengers were not allowed to land until just before five. Frenchtown consisted of one large house, its outbuildings, and a warehouse. Two stages and a wagon for luggage left Frenchtown at half past five for the four-hour trip to New Castle. After an hour and a half in New Castle, during which he explored the town and had a meal, the traveler boarded the packet boat to Philadelphia. Four boats sailed the New Castle-Philadelphia route. Two were considered to be the fastest on the river, making the journey in less than three hours under the best conditions. This man's trip took five hours, plus waiting another hour to land in Philadelphia's busy harbor. The entire expedition took two days.[16]

Until the introduction of new means of transportation in the early nineteenth century, the journey itself did not change much, but the ownership of it did. In 1775, Joseph Tatlow of New Castle owned and operated the route from Philadelphia to Frenchtown, while someone else ran the boats on the Chesapeake. Whether Tatlow continued to be involved in the 1790s is unknown, but several other New Castle men owned packet boats then. In 1806, however, William McDonald and Andrew Henderson, both of Maryland, owned and operated the entire Baltimore-Philadelphia route, while Edward Trippe ran a rival line between Courthouse Point on the Maryland side and Port Penn on the Delaware. Each line had three boats on the Delaware and four on the Chesapeake. On land, twelve two-ton wagons and four coaches were used every day. Depending on the weather, service was offered six days a week. Although both lines were doing well, the situation was not necessarily good for New Castle: the rival line went to Port Penn and outsiders owned the New Castle line.[17]

A canal across the peninsula, dreamed of for many years, promised to become reality with the formation of the Chesapeake and Delaware Canal Company in 1803. The project was a regional venture with directors divided equally among Pennsylvania, Maryland, and Delaware. One man came from New Castle. Great debate arose over the canal's eastern end point. New Castle hoped to be the chosen place. Benjamin Henry Latrobe, who surveyed the route, did

*Chapter 3 – A Town Among Cities*

favor New Castle, but stock sales and politics did not. New Castle's hopes were dashed when the directors decided to terminate the canal in the Christina, which would give Wilmington the major advantage. In the end, however, no one profited, for the company ran out of money soon after beginning to dig and abandoned the project.[18]

Providing government was the other major component of New Castle's economy and urban identity. Although no longer the state

Town Hall and Market, *Robert Montgomery Bird, watercolor, 1826.*
*This rare view shows the rear of Town Hall, erected in the early 1820s, and the market house extending behind it.*
*(Courtesy of Robert Montgomery Bird and The Winterthur Library: Decorative Arts Photographic Collection.)*

capital, it was still the seat of New Castle County and the site of Delaware sessions of federal courts. Until 1811, the entire county voted at New Castle.[19] Some townspeople, such as lawyers, public officials, and those who provided goods and services to the county, profited directly from the presence of government. Government business, especially on election day and during court sessions, also brought outsiders to town, who might shop or stop for a drink or a meal. While townspeople could do little to promote this feature, they would learn through hard experience that they had to fight simply to retain this source of profit and prestige.

The port, transportation services, and county seat were New Castle's means to profit and status, but the town also had the other normal features of an urban economy: taverns, craftsmen, merchants, and, after 1807, a branch of the state's bank. New Castle's craft sector provided mainly the skills and products needed in daily life. Except for a few cabinetmakers and one clockmaker, there were no luxury trades, but such items were easily available in Wilmington or Philadelphia. Shipbuilding was conspicuously absent. Nevertheless, between 1796 and 1799 and again in 1804 and 1805, the town had a printer, a sure sign of urban aspiration and promise. In 1804 and 1805, it even had a newspaper, the *New Castle Argus*.[20]

Taverns naturally were an important feature of an economy based on moving goods and people and providing government services. They ranged form John Darragh's "Sign of the Ship and Pilot-Boat," advertising the "GENTEELEST ENTERTAINMENT," to unlicensed dives serving "itinerant merchants, apprentice boys, negroes and mulattoes of both sexes, and rogues and blackguards of every description."[21] In 1799, New Castle Hundred had twelve licensed houses, second in the county to Christiana Hundred's (Wilmington) seventeen; the next highest hundred had seven.[22]

Although New Castle was not a major commercial center, its mercantile sector was vigorous and ambitious. At least a dozen firms of small to intermediate size dealt mainly in dry goods and groceries at various times during the period. In addition, the town boasted a drugstore and a bookstore. Bond and Lees, the largest firm, operated between 1789 and 1794, and fit into the mold of the generalist eighteenth-century merchant. The firm bought and sold a wide variety of items. It also owned ships in the coastal trade, at least a share of the New Castle–Philadelphia packet boats, and property in New Castle and the surrounding countryside. Although Bond and Lees apparently did not trade directly with Europe, it did have an office in Philadelphia.[23] The patterns of New Castle's trade are obscure. Most merchants probably bought their stock in Wilmington or Philadelphia. They obviously sold to townspeople and the ship-supply trade, but how far their market extended into the surrounding area is unknown. New Castle merchants certainly aspired to a wider market, for they advertised in Wilmington newspapers.

New Castle's new vigor and ambition led to struggle with Wilmington. Rivalry between them was not new, but it now became public, using, at various times, the press, state government, political parties, and even the federal government, whereas earlier rivalry had been more informal and private. A powerful emotional element accompanied the competition for trade and profit. By 1800, New Castle had seen its place usurped by both Philadelphia and Wilmington, and it hurt. As John Munroe so aptly expressed it, the town was "nurturing its pride and its grudges beside the river."[24]

The first battle in the interurban war began in 1801 with Wilmington's plan to build a drawbridge over the Christina River at Market Street. In order to do this, the Wilmington Bridge Company needed a corporate charter, which could be granted only by the Delaware General Assembly. New Castle feared that this improvement—the first bridge over the Christina—would lead people to use it to go to Wilmington to do their business, rather than taking existing roads that led to New Castle. This set the stage for a lengthy struggle that involved petitions to the legislature, newspaper articles for and against the bridge, threats to move the county seat, charges that Philadelphia was behind New Castle's protests, party politics, and accusations that New Castle was acting deviously and selfishly, while Wilmington was acting from purely local interests. New Castle managed to delay the project, but the Wilmington Bridge Company received its charter in 1807.[25]

By 1807, New Castle, no longer run down and depressed, had experienced nearly a decade and a half of sustained prosperity and success. Quite a few new houses had been built, including some on "Speculation Alley."[26] George Read II's mansion overlooking the river was the epitome of elegance. The Episcopalians and Presbyterians undertook major improvements to their churches and the Roman Catholics began to build their place of worship. The dreams of town government and piers in the river became reality in the mid-1790s. The ambitious town fathers commissioned Benjamin Henry Latrobe's elaborate survey of the town and planned major street improvements. The Trustees of the Common began to fulfill their goal of using their land to benefit the town, with the funding of the handsome Academy on the Green as their first major project. Economic energy and success bred civic spirit.

In comparison with what was to come, and what had been, New Castle's success between the early 1790s and 1807 came easily. The town had exploded into life and felt confident that it could achieve further success in the future. Real estate advertisements included glowing descriptions of New Castle's advantages and prospects for the only time in the sixty years of this study.[27] The Wilmington Bridge battle brought a taste of reality, however. New Castle's leaders learned that they could not entirely control their world, and that enacting their dreams of being more than a sleepy village would often require hard fighting. The combination of prosperity and initiation into rough-and-tumble urban warfare provided New Castle with a secure base for more difficult times ahead.

*Chapter 3 – A Town Among Cities*

## WELL-TEMPERED OPTIMISM, 1808–1828

The buoyant prosperity was not to last, however, for New Castle had little control over many of the forces and events that would shape its world. Between 1808 and 1828, the town strove and fought with mixed results. Achievements included the drawbridge at Newport, steamboats on the river, a turnpike to Frenchtown, a secure county seat, the beginnings of railroad development, and many signs of civic and religious vigor. Underneath lay problems, however. The population, which had increased between 1800 and 1810, actually declined from 1,021 in 1810 to 996 in 1830. In correspondence, people often said that New Castle was dull; no one commented on its prosperity or glowing prospects.

External factors limited the port: the Embargo of 1808 and the War of 1812; Philadelphia's loss of commercial primacy to New York;

*Detail from* New Castle Waterfront, *Robert Shaw, watercolor, 1896. Robert Shaw (1859–1912) of Wilmington liked to preserve Delaware's disappearing past through his art. This work is Shaw's copy of a painting of New Castle found on a panel from a Delaware River steamboat. It depicts the town around 1830. (Courtesy of the Historical Society of Delaware.)*

the decline in the relative importance of foreign trade in the nation's economy; and the gradual shift in the region's economic orientation from foreign trade to industry. Gone were any hopes or pretensions of being even a small commercial center; gone too, at least from extant sources, is any indication of an active ship supply trade. New Castle, however, continued to function as a refuge; in January and February, fourteen to seventeen vessels might anchor there.[28] Indeed, the harbor may have been busiest during the off-season.

New Castle's citizens did not see the harbor as a focal point in this period; instead, it gradually filled with mud. As early as 1811, James McCallmont, who held the ferry franchise, found that his 130-foot-long wharf, erected ten years earlier, was so trapped in mud that the ferries could not land. He planned to extend the wharf 60 feet, even longer if necessary. Mud continued to accumulate; in 1817, McCallmont and the Trustees of the Common jointly built a new public wharf 310 feet long. By the mid-1820s the harbor was nearly unusable, if some writers are to be believed; indeed, the question of the harbor's safety and accessibility led to a brief skirmish in the war with Wilmington. Finally, in 1827, Congress appropriated money for harbor improvements.[29]

Continuing to capitalize on the flow of people and goods up and down the coast, New Castle's men put most of their economic energy into developing the regional transportation network, building on existing packet and stage lines. As the nineteenth century began, transportation was wretched, but improvements were soon to come. The new innovations—turnpikes, steamboats, canals, and railroads—came so quickly that the early nineteenth century has been labeled the "Transportation Revolution." Each one affected New Castle.

New Castle did not accept its defeat in the Wilmington Bridge battle as final, and responded in 1808 with a plan to build a bridge over the Christina River at Newport, a few miles downriver from Wilmington. The Trustees of the Common were deeply involved in the project. In 1812, they solicited plans for the bridge, and the next

## Chapter 3 – A Town Among Cities

year they appointed a "Draw Bridge Committee" and paid the expenses of a lobbyist sent to Dover. Three of the five commissioners named in the bridge's charter were Trustees.[30]

The campaign to obtain a state charter touched off a fight similar to that over the Wilmington Bridge. The arguments against the bridge were familiar: there were already other roads in the area, navigation of the Christina would be impeded, the bridge would be useless if the county seat were moved, and the existing ferry at Newport was not heavily used. As with the earlier battle, this one involved more than bridges. In 1809, bridge supporters were accused of resorting to shady tricks to insure that they would have a strong voice in the legislature. Their ploy was to nominate, on the majority Republican ticket, a New Castle Hundred man who would run, win, and resign, so that the vacancy could be filled by a special election. The first part of the stratagem worked, but the second did not; the bridge supporter was defeated in the special election and the charter was not granted until 1813. Another holdover from the first battle was a movement in 1809 to change the county seat. The strongest language was reserved for moral judgments; New Castle was accused of being selfish and unethical, of promoting the Newport Bridge solely to strike back at Wilmington and to provide a profit for a few.[31] As one writer eloquently expressed it, after the Wilmington Bridge became reality, "the New-Castle leaders were left to suffer the contempt of their betrayed confederates, and, like debauched gamesters, already ruined at play, instead of turning their attention to industry and economy, to plunge madly into new excesses, to divert the attention of the public from their past enormities and to drown the recollection of lost confidence."[32] As with the Wilmington Bridge, the opposition only caused a delay; the Newport Bridge Company received its charter in 1813.[33]

The Newport Bridge battle coincided with the heyday of turnpike construction in the area, and New Castle was involved in this as well. In 1809 and 1810 the Delaware and Maryland legislatures chartered the New Castle and Frenchtown Turnpike Company, authorized to improve the busy but terrible road to Frenchtown. The proposed turnpike apparently aroused the envy and anger of New Castle's neighbors. These feelings were premature, however, for the company failed to raise enough capital to organize and then fell dormant. Undeterred, New Castle men organized a more modest venture in 1811, a two-mile turnpike from New Castle to Clark's Corner (Hare's Corner), which succeeded. Stock ownership was evenly distributed; fifty-six people bought five shares each and one bought ten. Many were local men, investing in hopes of helping their town's overall prospects rather than for direct personal profit. The road was finished late in the summer of 1812 and began to pay dividends in 1813.[34]

The Newport Bridge Company also became involved in turnpikes. Since bridge tolls could not be collected until the road from the bridge to New Castle had been improved, and since both the bridge and the road were too much for it to handle, the company arranged for the New Castle Turnpike Company to build the road. The bridge company owned two-thirds of the additional stock issued for this purpose, or about 30 percent of the turnpike company's total stock. The road from the Newport Bridge to Clark's Corner was finished in 1816; the bridge presumably was completed by then, too.[35]

Meanwhile, the Union Line, a consolidation of the two rival firms that had earlier provided boats, wagons, and coaches on the route, brought another of the era's innovations, the steamboat, to New Castle around 1813. Although the firm took in New Castle's John and Thomas Janvier as partners around this time, most of its owners were not local. With its new-fangled steamboats and heavy use of the road to Frenchtown, this outside organization would be a potent force in New Castle's transportation developments.[36]

Although the New Castle and Frenchtown Turnpike's charter had lapsed, the need for an improved road had not disappeared. No one was more aware of it than the Union Line, which pushed the turnpike company to renew its charter in 1813. By now, conditions were more favorable: the New Castle Turnpike set a successful precedent, traffic was increasing, and the Union Line promised a high volume of business. This time the company succeeded; the turnpike was finished in 1816. The Union Line continued to play a major role in its fortunes, for the line's wagons and coaches provided a great deal of traffic and income.[37]

Despite battles and setbacks, by 1816 New Castle's links in the regional transportation network were complete and up to date. The town could regard its accomplishments with pride and hope. That so much had been achieved despite the national disruptions of 1808 to 1815, which destroyed the trade that previously had been the source of New Castle's prosperity, shows the town's strength, confidence, and optimism. The turnpike companies, with the help of heavy Union Line traffic, did reasonably well, usually breaking even and often paying dividends. They were more successful than many turnpikes and were the basis for the railroad built in the late 1820s and early 1830s. The Union Line also did well, although it had to combat competition. The Newport Bridge was a flop; by 1827 the company was deeply in debt and the New Castle Turnpike Company abandoned its turnpike to Newport.[38]

Two new developments of the 1820s, the canal boom and the railroad, all too soon challenged New Castle's facilities. Philadelphians revived the dormant Chesapeake and Delaware Canal Company in the early 1820s in hopes of providing easier access to the Maryland market, thus expanding the city's hinterland and strengthening its position in relation to New York. This time the canal was primarily by and for Philadelphia rather than a regional venture. Neither New Castle nor Wilmington liked the idea since the canal would be cheaper and more convenient than existing routes and its eastern end would be at Delaware City. New Castle was especially concerned lest the Union Line forsake it for the canal. As the canal showed signs of becoming reality, both New Castle and Wilmington investigated railroads as a way of offsetting the threat. Although there was some talk of a joint venture, in the end each town acted on its own. With the encouragement of the Union Line, New Castle decided to build its railroad along the New Castle and Frenchtown route and received its charter in 1829, before Wilmington. New Castle had bested its rival, or so it seemed.[39]

It is almost impossible to gauge the effects of transportation development on New Castle's economy in terms of dollars or jobs; the records do not exist. The turnpikes probably did not make anyone's fortune, while much of the Union Line's profit went to outsiders. Travelers obviously spent money in New Castle's shops and taverns. Many of the jobs generated by transportation required few specialized skills. The only extant figures suggest that the volume of traffic was volatile: in 1827, Union Line coaches made 2,853 trips; in 1828, 5,216; in 1829, 4,438; and 2,934 in 1830.[40] The last figure probably reflects traffic diverted to the newly opened canal. Such fluctuations obviously affected profits and employment. Nevertheless, transportation kept the town busy, even if it did not generate great wealth.

New Castle's hold on the county seat was secure after the Newport Bridge battle was over, but its governmental role was diminished in another way. In 1811, Delaware was divided into election districts for the first time. People no longer had to travel to their county seat to vote but cast their ballots in their own hundreds. To add insult to injury, New Castle Hundred's polling place was moved from the courthouse to a tavern about two miles from town. New Castle lost the excitement, status, and economic benefit that came from hosting elections and the county's electors, numbering between 1,700 and 2,400, who came to town. In 1823, however, the hundred's polling place was moved back to the courthouse.[41]

The town's craft and mercantile sectors also faced up to limitations that can be summed up in one fact: before 1808, merchants and craftsmen advertised fairly regularly in the Wilmington papers; after 1808, they did not. New Castle's market had shifted; while earlier businessmen competed with Wilmington for trade, their successors had to be content with mainly local custom.

Three of life's great calamities, war, economic depression, and fire, punctuated New Castle's experience between 1808 and 1828. The Embargo of 1808 and the War of 1812 destroyed the active foreign trade that brought prosperity to New Castle, but the town did not crumble into depression. Instead, energy and money were invested in the development of regional transportation improvements. This major reorientation of the town's economy coincided with the War of 1812. The war brought fear, loss, and trauma, but the town was not attacked or damaged and its economy was neither made nor unmade.

Although the nation enjoyed a boom for about three years after the end of the War of 1812, Philadelphia and its region did not share in it. During the first decade of the nineteenth century, that city permanently lost its position as America's primary port to New York, and then began to develop its manufacturing potential, producing for the regional market. The end of the war and the influx of British goods depressed the young industrial sector before it was firmly established.[42] When the Panic of 1819 "officially" arrived, Philadelphia had already experienced several bad years, caught in the vulnerable transition between a commercial and a manufacturing economy.

Detailed information is unavailable for Wilmington, but its condition was probably similar, for it too had manufacturing and commercial sectors. In late 1817, one newspaper writer said that although the city had many natural advantages and the potential to be active and prosperous, it was currently stagnating. He felt that Philadelphia wanted to keep Wilmington in a subordinate position.[43]

New Castle apparently shared in the region's postwar stagnation, but the signs and effects of hard times can be detected only indirectly. In early 1818, the author of a scheme to unite Delaware with Maryland said that "it would give life and animation to that place [New Castle] such as it has hitherto been stranger to."[44]

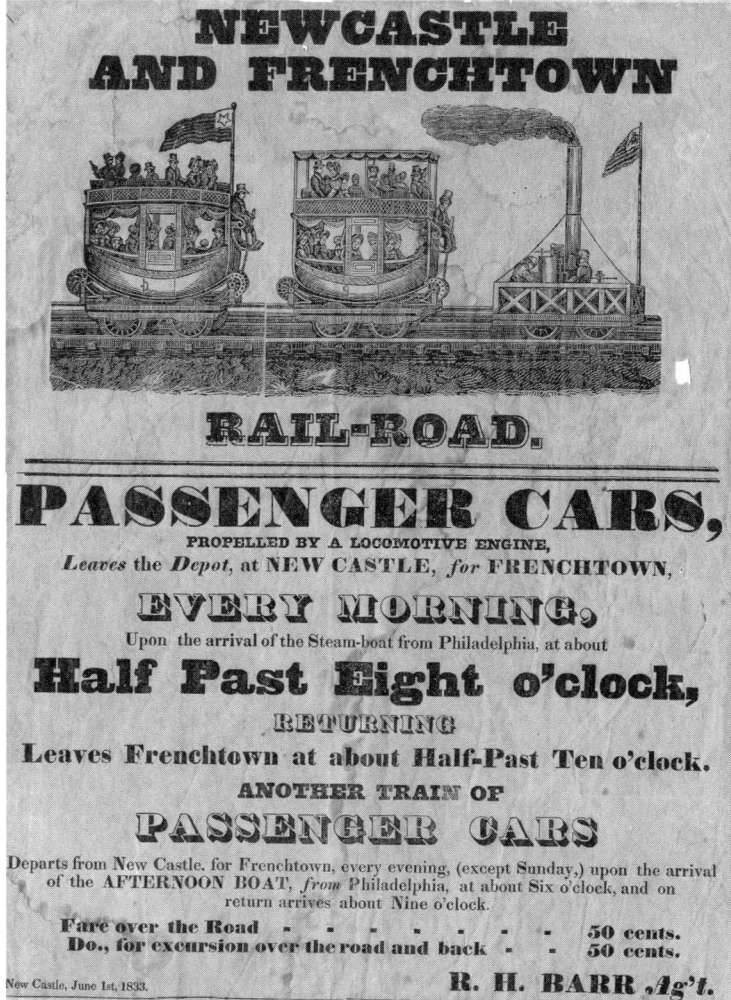

*New Castle and Frenchtown Rail-Road, June 1, 1833. The cars resemble stagecoaches rather than modern railroad cars. (Courtesy of the Historical Society of Delaware.)*

## Chapter 3 – A Town Among Cities

Demography offers the strongest hint: in 1820, the population was almost exactly what it had been ten years earlier.

On April 26, 1824, fire destroyed over half of the Strand (then called Water Street), New Castle's waterfront street and main commercial center. The fire broke out around two or three in the afternoon in James Riddle's stable at the south end of the street and soon spread to an adjoining lumberyard. With the aid of a strong south wind, the fire raced up both sides of the street, destroying homes and businesses in its path. Everyone, including women, fought the flames, carrying water and trying to save what they could. Furniture was stashed in the Market House, the Arsenal, the Presbyterian Church, and the street. Fire engines and about 400 men from Wilmington rushed to New Castle's assistance; without their help, the fire would have been worse. By midnight, the flames were nearly subdued, but the wind then switched to the northeast and again the alarm went out. Rain the next afternoon finally extinguished the fire.[45] As one newspaper article reported, "Never have we seen a spectacle more distressing, than this once beautiful town now presents.—From the north to the south end on Water Street, little is to be soon but tottering walls and solitary chimneys, and this section of the place, which was once the theatre of business, is now abandoned, and left a solitary heap of ruin and desolation."[46] Twenty-three families were homeless, left with little more than the clothes that they wore. Eight craftsmen, eight merchants, and three innkeepers lost their businesses. The loss was estimated at $100,000–200,000. Even so, the tragedy could have been greater, for no lives were lost.[47]

People immediately began to rebuild their lives and their town. A town meeting on April 28 set up a fund to raise money to help the victims. Donations came from Philadelphia, Boston, Washington, New York, and Baltimore, as well as Delaware towns. Even in this time of need, the New Castle-Wilmington rivalry continued; despite pleas for generosity, Wilmingtonians contributed only $572 of the

$7,630 that was raised. The fund covered only a small portion of the loss; people depended mainly on their own resources.[48]

By July 1824, reconstruction was progressing quickly. As one newspaper put it, probably with exaggeration: "New Castle has recently been visited by an extensive conflagration, but by the benevolent contributions of other citizens, and the spirit of her own, she has risen, more than Phoenix like from her ashes; the houses burned, have been rebuilt, and the town improved, in appearance at least."[49] The new buildings were conservative in style, fitting in well with two surviving structures, George Read II's house and Charles Thomas's hotel. At a time when they could have made changes, people chose the safe and the familiar.[50]

On the whole, New Castle's people handled their economic situation between 1808 and 1828 with persistence, vigor, and moderate success. They switched from foreign trade to transportation and were not afraid to use new innovations. These years were also marked by continuing civic and religious development. Especially in religion, horizons widened to include women, children, and blacks more fully in the community. Nevertheless, the accomplishments did not come easily or quickly and success was not overwhelming. Already there were hints that New Castle would not grow to rival Wilmington: population stagnation, mud in the river, threats to the county seat, and the feeling that New Castle was a dull place. Yet on the whole, New Castle did well, especially considering that the general economic situation between 1808 and 1821 was not good and the region was in the beginning of a major transition. Whatever their secret doubts, New Castle's men faced the world with outward confidence at the end of the 1820s—after all, they were about to build a railroad.

## Digging In, 1828–1840

Between 1828 and 1840, New Castle had some of the appearance, promise, and reality of prosperity and increasing stature, but the final result was stagnation. The railroad and the New Castle

## Chapter 3 – A Town Among Cities

Manufacturing Company, one of the nation's first makers of locomotive engines, were New Castle's last new ventures in this period. Their success was brief and New Castle was increasingly on the defensive, trying to preserve its assets from what it saw as Wilmington's greed. In the late 1830s, the town lost its advantages as a transportation center and barely retained the county seat. The world was closing in; New Castle was learning its limitations, trying hard to combat them, and getting nowhere fast.

The New Castle and Frenchtown Railroad became the centerpiece of the town's economy. With state charters to build a railroad across the peninsula, the New Castle Turnpike Company and the New Castle and Frenchtown Turnpike Company set out to raise capital. The first attempt failed, but the second, in March 1830, succeeded. New Castle people invested heavily, as did men in Philadelphia and Baltimore. The companies then merged, calling the new entity the New Castle and Frenchtown Turnpike and Railroad Company. Ten of the fourteen directors were from New Castle, with two each from Frenchtown and Baltimore. New Castle's John and Thomas Janvier, deeply involved in the Union Line, were on the board. By the next annual meeting, in May 1831, however, Philadelphia stockholders were dissatisfied with the project's progress. Four Philadelphians joined the board. They increased the speed and efficiency of construction, hoping to complete the railroad by 1832 in order to compete with the canal, which had opened in 1829.[51]

With the exception of the Chesapeake and Delaware Canal, the railroad was the largest project undertaken in Delaware up to that time. By April 1831, 1,100 men were employed and more were needed. As work progressed, the directors faced problems of bad weather, obtaining supplies, and ever-increasing costs. They faced the additional challenge of building one of the nation's first railroads. There were also disputes among the directors. As with the turnpikes, the Janviers were a major source of friction; by November 1831, both had sold their stock and resigned from the board. With the Janviers out, two Philadelphia men, William. B. Lewis and S. Nevins, became the strongest voices on the board. They had doubts about New Castle; as one of them wrote from the town, "I rejoice that I remain here, I am afraid to trust too much to N Castle Men."[52]

Finally, the problems were surmounted and the railroad opened in late February 1832, but with trains drawn by horses rather than by a steam locomotive. The first train arrived safely at Frenchtown after a trip of about one hour and twenty minutes, considerably faster than the stagecoach. At year's end, the directors were pleased: passenger and freight business was good, and two steam engines had replaced horses.[53]

Even with the railroad, the journey from Philadelphia to Baltimore via New Castle and Frenchtown still required two segments by water. Without reliable steamboat service, the railroad went nowhere, and this was a major concern for the company. At first, the railroad had a favorable arrangement with the Citizens Union Line, which had absorbed the old Union Line by the end of 1830. But to make its position more secure the New Castle and Frenchtown obtained permission to own steamboats, and promptly merged with the Citizens Union Line in April 1833. This put the entire route under one ownership, but most of the money and leadership came from Philadelphia and Baltimore rather than New Castle.[54]

The New Castle and Frenchtown flourished until 1837, although not without forebodings of future problems, namely the construction and uniting of the Wilmington and Susquehanna Railroad and its three companion roads into the Philadelphia, Wilmington and Baltimore Railroad. The New Castle and Frenchtown did what it could to thwart the competition. When the Wilmington and Susquehanna made its second and successful attempt to raise capital in 1835, the Wilmington papers accused the New Castle and Frenchtown of working in Philadelphia to discourage investment. Nevertheless, the stock sold quickly. A little later, in July 1835, the Delaware General Assembly held a special session to enact a law repairing defects in the Wilmington and Susquehanna's charter. The New Castle and Frenchtown's opposition was so strong and venomous that it was totally ineffective; the law passed unanimously in both houses.[55]

Once the Wilmington and Susquehanna, and hence the through railroad between Philadelphia and Baltimore, approached reality, "citizens of Delaware"—really citizens of New Castle—petitioned the legislature in September 1836 for permission to build a railroad from New Castle to join the Wilmington and Susquehanna. Although Philadelphia men supported the project, Wilmington of course did not, accusing New Castle of greedily attempting to take advantage of its neighbor's hard work. The battle continued for several years, ending with the chartering of the New Castle and Wilmington Railroad Company in 1839. The short road, however, was not built until 1854.[56]

Meanwhile, the Philadelphia, Wilmington and Baltimore Railroad opened in late 1837, providing, for the first time, fast, direct transportation between Philadelphia and Baltimore, and ending the New Castle and Frenchtown's dreams of success and domination of peninsular transportation. In February 1839, a "large amount" of New Castle and Frenchtown stock was transferred to the Philadelphia, Wilmington and Baltimore and in 1843 the two companies received permission to mange their affairs jointly. The New Castle and Frenchtown maintained its name but not its independence; New Castle was truly a town among cities. Although New Castle fought long and hard in the transportation battle, its dominance was never secure, it never fully controlled the means of using its route, and in the end it was vanquished by a more creative use of new technology and the money, power, and more favorable locations of its larger neighbors.[57]

The railroad, plus the increasing practicability of steam power, pushed New Castle's economy in a new direction: for the first time, it turned to manufacturing for a market greater than purely local needs.

The product was railroad engines. The New Castle and Frenchtown had facilities for repairing its rolling stock and also the good fortune to hire an extremely talented engineer; the next step was to make entire engines. Five were completed in the railroad's shops in 1834 and 1835. Meanwhile, a group of New Castle men received a charter for the New Castle Manufacturing Company in January 1833. The company appears to have been operating by summer 1835. In 1836, it produced eight engines, and one each in 1838, 1839, and 1840. The depression of the late 1830s was hard on the company; production and employment fell sharply and it had severe money problems.[58] This newspaper article gives the fullest description of the firm:

> The capacious buildings; the powerful and ingenious machinery; the order, regularity, and neatness throughout the establishment are highly creditable to the judgment and enterprise of the company and its superintendants. We feel emotions of pride, in knowing that such a large manufactory of steam engines exists in our State. The loco motives [*sic*] built by this company have been proved by constant and heavy duty to be of most superior workmanship and the best materials; and wherever they are used they give the fullest satisfaction. A vast amount of work has been executed in this establishment, which at one time gave employment to one hundred and fifty workmen; but at present not much more than one–third of that number are engaged; the dullness of the times has stricken this house of industry and enterprize, and many a wheel is stationary and many a hammer silent.[59]

With a peak work force of one hundred fifty, the New Castle Manufacturing Company must have been a large and impressive establishment at a time when factory production was still new. The firm continued to produce into the late 1850s.

The railroad and manufacturing company never occupied all of New Castle's attention; older concerns and activities continued to be important. The harbor continued to serve as a winter auxiliary for Philadelphia, although still plagued with the traditional problems of mud and Wilmington. During the mid-to-late 1830s the harbor received a great deal of attention. By early 1835 it was again so filled with mud that ships could not anchor, and townspeople asked the federal government to build still more piers. About a year later, some Wilmingtonians suggested that the Christina should become Philadelphia's winter harbor, claiming that New Castle was unsafe and that no amount of money could cure the mud problem. In the end, New Castle remained Philadelphia's winter refuge and new piers were authorized in 1836. The planned railroad to Wilmington would also help the harbor, for ships stopping at New Castle could unload and send the cargo to Philadelphia by rail rather than awaiting favorable sailing conditions. Philadelphia merchants gave the project strong moral support, but the fact that the road was not completed until 1854 suggests that they did not invest in it.[60]

In the mid 1830s, New Castle again campaigned to be made a port of entry with the same customs authority as Wilmington. The campaign was well organized: New Castle sent petitions and committees to the nation's capital, as well as using the services of William

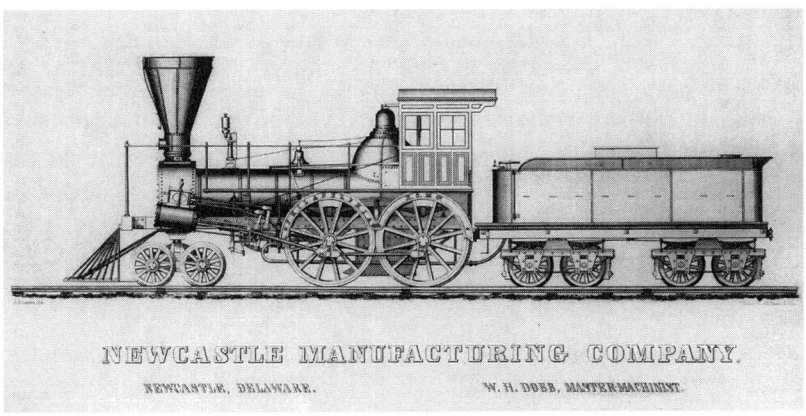

*"Philadelphia," engine built by the New Castle Manufacturing Company, 1852. (Courtesy of the Historical Society of Delaware.)*

T. Read, a local man working in the Treasury Department. Philadelphia and other Delaware towns gave their support. Although the government considered New Castle's request unusual and unorthodox since most customs districts had only one port of entry, it also felt that New Castle had a legitimate grievance and agreed to station a deputy collector there, who had assumed his duties by 1839.[61]

The harbor was indeed busy during the winter. In the first three months of 1839 over one hundred vessels sought refuge. The next winter, ninety-four visited the port; about a third stayed one day or less, but a quarter stayed a week or longer. With improvements, even more would stop, for in 1840, the harbor offered only partial protection.[62] What this meant for New Castle's economy is a difficult question. A full harbor would give the appearance of activity and prosperity during the bleak winter months, but ships staying only a day or two would not spend much money in town. The harbor's activity depended on the volume of trade being done at Philadelphia as well as that city's wishes and support.

The Newport Bridge continued to be a dead weight. The company frequently tried to persuade New Castle County to buy the bridge, but without success. The county had reservations because of the company's debts, the bridge's bad condition, and doubts about the sale's legality. Even after the bridge company had a law passed confirming the sale's validity, the county refused. The issue was briefly an important concern in New Castle Hundred. Late in 1831, ninety-five men signed a petition requesting that the hundred be incorporated, mainly so that it could buy, repair, and operate the bridge, since the county seemed unwilling to do so. Fifty-six signed a petition against the proposal. The last glimpse of the bridge comes in 1836, when the county again declined to buy it.[63]

Along with the railroad, the biggest issue of the 1830s was the prolonged battle over the county seat. Interurban rivalry was at its height: New Castle naturally wanted to keep the courts, Wilmington wanted to acquire them, and the rest of the county took sides. The

Chapter 3 – A Town Among Cities

decision was to be made through a special county election. Since it took four attempts to pass the enabling act in the legislature, followed by the election itself, meetings and propaganda flourished.[64]

From a practical, reasonably objective point of view, Wilmington's supporters had a strong case. Both demography and economics made the city more convenient, they claimed, and facts were in their favor. About two-thirds of the county's adult white males lived north of the Christina, and Wilmington, larger and busier than New Castle, offered more opportunities for transacting business. New Castle had been off the beaten track for thirty years in their estimation. The public buildings at New Castle were a disgrace: parts of the courthouse were leaky and drafty, the jail was notoriously insecure, and government records were stored in garrets. Something needed to be done; since Wilmington had offered to provide some of the needed facilities, a move would not be expensive. Taxes would not be raised and the county would profit from selling the old buildings. Although such changes in basic institutions should not be made often or quickly, in this case public opinion and convenience justified the move. The people's wishes should be followed; county seats had been changed in other states and even in Delaware's Sussex County.

New Castle supporters' arguments naturally were the opposite, and had, in truth, less factual basis. Those who favored New Castle's location came from less densely populated areas. Also, New Castle simply lacked Wilmington's shops and business facilities. While not denying the sorry state of the courthouse and jail, New Castle supporters doubted the sincerity of Wilmington's offer and predicted increased taxes. Repairing existing buildings would be less expensive; it was even suggested that the Common be asked to pay for the renovations. New Castle supporters claimed that the people did not want the courts moved, at least not before a selfish minority in Wilmington stirred up the issue, but an 1835 petition campaign yielded 2,300 signatures in favor of a change and only 1,100 against. The county seat had always been at New Castle and it should remain; a few essentially said that it was divinely ordained.

Emotional, speculative, and moral arguments proliferated and intertwined. A favorite theme was the potential effect of the move on New Castle. Moving the courts would bring economic devastation, with declining property values and a loss of business for shops, hotels, and the bank. It would also lead to a loss of population and a decline in civic spirit, New Castle's supporters said.[65] The economic speculations were confined to New Castle. Wilmington's motivation for wanting the county seat was not primarily, or at least not overtly, economic; rather, it was a matter of convenience, prestige, logic, and local rivalry. The next question was, which place deserved the distinction. Wilmington supporters felt that the courts naturally belonged in the county's largest and busiest city; they thought that New Castle should give up gracefully rather than cling desperately to its last vestige of former importance.

Both sides fought hard, with petitions, meetings, printed propaganda, and lobbyists. New Castle even established a newspaper in 1835 to provide ammunition. It did not last long and very few issues survive. The Common funded lobbyists on three separate occasions. New Castle's efforts helped to postpone passage of the law authorizing the election until 1839, and some contended that the procedures favored New Castle. The day of reckoning came in May 1839; when it was over, New Castle had retained the county seat by the skin of its teeth.[66]

In this difficult period, the general economic climate was favorable until the Panic of 1837 and subsequent depression arrived in the midst of the county seat battle and just as the town was face to face with the new and damaging Philadelphia, Wilmington and Baltimore Railroad. The emotional impact must have been tremendous; the actual effect is almost impossible to assess. New Castle's population grew slightly between 1830 and 1840, probably because of the railroad and manufacturing company. By the late 1830s, both

## Chapter 3 – A Town Among Cities

enterprises were in trouble, and New Castle probably had a high rate of unemployment.

In 1835 the *New Castle Gazette* published an editorial lauding the town's advantages—its improving spirit, Delaware River location, easy communications with the rest of the nation, easy access to raw materials, markets, and surrounding agricultural areas, and the harbor with federally-funded improvements—and ending with an optimistic prediction for the future: "Under the guidance of judicious enterprise, and with such advantages and others which might be enumerated, New-Castle cannot fail to become, ere long, what Nature evidently intended she should be—the seat of large and successful Manufacturing business." [67] Appearances can deceive, however, and New Castle's people must have known that their town was not going to rival Wilmington. As one man wrote, also in 1835, "the manufacturing company George mentioned as about going into operations will I hope help our town"—hardly an enthusiastic vote of confidence.[68] Activity abounded during the 1830s, but with little long-term or substantial effect. The railroad flourished only briefly; even in its best days, local people did not fully own and manage it. The Newport Bridge was a continuing irritant. The harbor was busy, but mainly during the winter and at Philadelphia's behest, while the manufacturing company foundered on the rocks of general hard times after a promising beginning. In the civic realm, town government and the Trustees of the Common maintained what they had and did not initiate any new ventures. Churches and religious organizations remained active, but in ways that emphasized differences and barriers rather than overcoming them. Interurban rivalry reached its peak during the lengthy county seat battle. At one point a newspaper even suggested that Wilmington and New Castle might some day be one city![69] The 1840 population of 1,061 was only 40 greater than it had been in 1810, hardly a sign of promise. Buffeted on many sides, New Castle turned inward to defend and protect what it had; by 1840 it had fought many a hard battle and learned a hard truth: it was destined to be only a town among cities.

[1] Diane Lindstrom, *Economic Development in the Philadelphia Region, 1810–1850* (New York, 1978), pp. 23, 29–40; Carol E. Hoffecker, "Nineteenth Century Wilmington: Satellite Or Independent City?" *Delaware History* 15 (1972): 4–7.

[2] C.A. Weslager, *Delaware's Forgotten River: The Story of the Christina* (Wilmington, 1947), pp. 147–65.

[3] *Delaware Gazette* (Wilmington; hereafter DelGaz), July 22, 1809.

[4] Johann David Schoepf, *Travels in the Confederation*, Alfred J. Morrison, trans. and ed. (Philadelphia, 1911), pp. 376–77.

[5] Curtis Clay to George Read, Oct. 29, 1787, Richard S. Rodney Collection, Historical Society of Delaware, Wilmington (hereafter HSD).

[6] Petition, citizens of the town of New Castle to the General Assembly, June 1786, Legislative Papers, Delaware Public Archives, Dover (hereafter DPA).

[7] Petitions, citizens of New Castle County to the General Assembly, Jan. 1786, and draft bill, "An Act to establish certain Free-Ports within the Delaware State, and for the Encouragement of Commerce," 1786, Legislative Papers, DPA; and John A. Munroe, *Federalist Delaware, 1775–1815* (New Brunswick, N.J., 1954), p. 133.

[8] Curtis P. Nettels, *The Emergence of a National Economy* (New York, 1962), pp. 60–63, 121, 232–36; and James Henretta, *The Evolution of American Society, 1700–1815: An Interdisciplinary Analysis* (Lexington, Mass., 1973), pp. 188–92.

[9] See Constance J. Cooper, "A Town Among Cities: New Castle, Delaware, 1780–1840" (Ph.D. dissertation, University of Delaware, 1983), chapter 4.

[10] Information on shipping at New Castle is sketchy; there are no customs or harbormaster's records, so the major source is occasional listings and advertisements in Wilmington newspapers. The harbor's activity is probably underestimated. Ships at New Castle, 1790–1797: 1790, 3 ships (DelGaz, Feb. 6, Nov. 20, 1790); 1792, 1 ship (DelGaz, Nov. 10, 1792); 1793, 3 ships (DelGaz, April 27, Sept. 5, 1793); 1794, 5 ships (Del.Gaz, May 3, Aug. 30, Sept. 13, 1794; *Delaware and Eastern Shore Advertiser* [Wilmington; hereafter DESA], July 19, Sept 3, 6, 1794); 1795, 1 ship (DESA, Oct. 31, 1795); 1796, 5 ships (DESA, Sept. 12, Nov. 24, 1796); 1797, 4 ships (DESA, Nov. 2, 1797; DelGaz, May 3, July 1, Aug. 2, 1797).

[11] Ships at New Castle, 1799–1807: 1799, 1 ship (DESA, Sept. 19, 1799); 1800, 3 ships *(Mirror of the Times* [Wilmington; hereafter Mirror], June 11, Sept.

## Chapter 3 – A Town Among Cities

10, 1800); 1801, 4 ships (Mirror, July 4, 1801, *Monitor* [Wilmington], Aug, 8, 1801); 1802, 6 ships (Mirror, June 5, 9, Aug, 14, 28, 1802); 1803, 4 ships (Mirror, July 27, Sept. 3, 1803, *Federal Ark* [Wilmington], Sept. 24, 1803); 1804, 8 ships *(Federal Ark,* Feb. 1, 8, 11, June 9, 1804); 1805, 9 ships (Mirror, Sept. 25, 1805; *New Castle Argus,* May 11, 15, June 4, 1805); 1807, 1 ship *(Museum of Delaware* [Wilmington; hereafter Museum], Jan. 3, 1807).

[12] George H. Gibson, ed., *The Collected Essays of Richard S. Rodney on Early Delaware* (Wilmington, 1975), p. 225; *Laws of the State of Delaware* (hereafter *Laws),* 3:223–28; William Read to George Read, Feb. 24, 1798 and June 11, 1802, George Read to James A. Bayard, Jan. 23, 1803, and Bayard to Read, Jan. 31, 1803, Richard S. Rodney Collection, HSD; "Report of the Committee of Manufactures...to whom was also referred, on the eleventh instant, a motion 'for the appropriation of —— dollars for the erection and repair of piers in the River Delaware'" (n.p, 1802); petition, citizens of the town of New Castle to the General Assembly, Dec. 31, 1802, Legislative Papers, DPA; and U.S. Congress, House, Port of Entry at New Castle, Delaware, *American State Papers: Commerce and Navigation,* 1:621–22.

[13] Robert C. Smith, ed., "A Portuguese Naturalist in Philadelphia, 1799," *Pennsylvania Magazine of History and Biography* 78 (1954): 75–76; Kenneth Roberts and Anna M. Roberts, eds. and trans., *Moreau de St. Méry's American Journey* (Garden City, N.Y., 1947), pp. 86–87; Joseph Scott, *A Geographical Description of the States of Maryland and Delaware; also of the counties, towns, rivers, bays, and islands* (Philadelphia, 1807), pp. 177–78; Duke de la Rochefoucauld-Liancourt, *Travels through the United States of North America, the country of the Iroquois, and Upper Canada, in the years, 1795, 1796, and 1797,* 2d ed., 4 vols. (London, 1800), 3:539; DESA, Sept, 15, 1796, Aug. 1, Sept. 19, 1799; and Mirror, Feb. 5, 1800, Sept. 15, 1802, Aug. 31, 1803.

[14] Harold B. Hancock, "Loaves and Fishes: Applications for Office from Delawareans to George Washington," *Delaware History* 14 (1970): 137.

[15] "A Statement Shewing the names, Ports, and Tonnage of Vessels belonging to the District of Delaware, and the Trade employed in—and distance from Port of Entry," undated, but probably late 1790s, DPA.

[16] Roberts and Roberts, *Moreau de St. Méry's American Journey,* pp. 82–89.

[17] William F. Holmes, "The New Castle and Frenchtown Turnpike and Railroad Company, 1809–1838" (M.A. thesis, University of Delaware, 1961), pp. 27–28; DESA, June 28, Oct. 25, 1794, Oct. 24, 1796; DelGaz, July 2, 1791, May 11, 1793; and U.S. Congress, Roads and Canals (Gallatin Report), *American State Papers: Miscellaneous,* 1:758.

[18] Ralph D. Gray, "Delaware and Its Canal: The Early History of the Chesapeake and Delaware Canal , 1769–1829" (M.A. thesis, University of Delaware, 1950), pp. 3, 32, 34–35, 42–57.

[19] David Paul Peltier, "Border State Democracy: A History of Voting in Delaware, 1682–1897" (Ph.D. dissertation, University of Delaware, 1967), pp. 130–38.

[20] Information on craftsmen comes from newspapers, estate inventories, and town tax records; Charles G. Dorman, "Delaware Cabinetmakers and Allied Artisans, 1655–1855," *Delaware History* 9 (1960): 111–217; Harold B. Hancock, "Furniture Craftsmen in Delaware Records," *Winterthur Portfolio* 9 (1974): 175–212; Evald Rink, *Printing in Delaware, 1761–1800* (Wilmington, 1969), p. 24; Clarence S. Brigham, *History and Bibliography of American Newspapers, 1690–1820*, 2 vols. (Worcester, Mass., 1927), 1:78; Ruthanna Hindes, *Delaware Silversmiths, 1700–1850* (Wilmington, 1967); and Dudley C. Lunt, *The Farmers Bank: An Historical Account of the President, Directors and Company of the Farmers Bank of the State of Delaware, 1807–1957* (The Farmers Bank of the State of Delaware, 1957), p. 3.

[21] DESA, June 24, 1795; and *New Castle Argus*, May 28, 1805.

[22] New Castle County Tavern Petitions, DPA.

[23] DESA, 1794– Sept. 1799 passim; DelGaz, 1786–1797 passim; Mirror, Feb. 1800–Oct. 1804 passim; and estate inventories of Thomas Smith (d. 1800), William Van Leuvenigh (d. 1800), Matthew McNight (d. 1805), William McClenahan (d. 1793), New Castle County Probate Records, DPA.

[24] Munroe, *Federalist Delaware*, p. 22.

[25] Petition, citizens of Wilmington to the General Assembly, 1801, and petitions to the General Assembly, 1804, 1805, 1806, Legislative Papers, DPA; James Lea et al. to C.A. Rodney, Jan. 26, July 9, 1802, Richard S. Rodney Collection, HSD; Mirror, March-May, 1803, passim, March-May 1806, passim, July 23, 1806; and Museum, Jan. 24, 1807.

[26] Mirror, Dec. 25, 1802.

[27] DelGaz, Aug. 30, 1799; DESA, Oct. 24, 1796; and Mirror, Dec. 25, 1802, March 15, May 14, 1803, April 7, 1804, Jan. 15, 1806.

[28] *American Watchman* (Wilmington; hereafter AmW), Feb. 20, 1813, Feb. 26, 1822; and DelGaz, Jan. 4, 8, 1822, Jan. 5, 1827.

[29] Petition from James McCallmont to the General Assembly, Jan. 16, 1811, and petition, citizens of the town of New Castle to the General Assembly, Jan. 1835, DPA; Minutes of the Trustees of the Common, pp. 105–6, held by Trustees of the Common (hereafter Common); and DelGaz, June 13, 1823.

[30] Petitions against bridge at Newport, 1808, Legislative Papers, DPA; Common, pp. 86–90; *Laws*, 4:650.

[31] DelGaz, July 1809–Jan. 1810 passim; AmW, Aug.–Sept 1809, passim; J. Clayton to George Read, Jan. 31, 1811, Richard S. Rodney Collection, HSD;

## Chapter 3 – A Town Among Cities

and petitions for removal of county seat, 1810, and against Newport Bridge, 1811–1813, Legislative Papers, DPA.

[32] DelGaz, July 26, 1809.

[33] *Laws,* 4:650–62.

[34] Ralph D. Gray, "Transportation and Brandywine Industries, 1800–1840," *Delaware History* 9 (1961): 310–11; Holmes, "New Castle and Frenchtown," pp. 32–37, 160–61; and DelGaz, July 22, 1809. Two-thirds of the fifty-seven investors can be found on the 1810 federal census for New Castle Hundred.

[35] Holmes, "New Castle and Frenchtown," p. 38; petition from the Newport Bridge Company to the General Assembly, April 5, 1813, Legislative papers, DPA; and *Laws,* 5:28–36.

[36] Holmes, "New Castle and Frenchtown," pp., 28, 39.

[37] Holmes, "New Castle and Frenchtown," pp. 39–46, 51–56, 60.

[38] Holmes, "New Castle and Frenchtown," pp. 48, 69, 120; John H.K. Shannahan, *Steamboat'n' Days & The Hammond Lot* (Baltimore, 1930), pp. 12–13; Levi Hollingsworth to George Read, Oct. 24, 1818, and Richard L. Howell to George Read, Dec. 12, 1818, Richard S. Rodney Collection, HSD; petition from proprietors of Union Line of Steam boats and packets to the General Assembly, Jan. 1820, Legislative papers, DPA; and New Castle County Levy Court minutes, March 1827, DPA.

[39] Gray, "Delaware and Its Canal," pp. 75–76; and Holmes, "New Castle and Frenchtown," pp. 71–81.

[40] Several memoranda regarding Union Line traffic, 1827–1830, are in the New Castle and Frenchtown Turnpike and Railroad Company Papers, HSD.

[41] Peltier, "Border State Democracy," pp. 130–38; Mirror, Oct. 11,1800, Oct. 10, 1801, Oct. 9, 1802; AmW, Oct. 7, 1809, Oct. 13, 1810; and *Laws,* 6:299.

[42] Anne Bezanson, Robert D. Gray, and Miriam Hussey, *Wholesale Prices in Philadelphia, 1784–1861* (Philadelphia, 1936), pp. 151–52.

[43] AmW, Dec. 1817–Feb. 1818 passim, esp. Dec. 17, 1817.

[44] AmW, Jan. 28, 1818.

[45] *Wilmingtonian,* April 29, 1824; DelGaz, April 27, 1824; and [Maria Booth Rogers] to James Rogers, [April 27, 1824], Boothurst Collection, HSD.

[46] *Wilmingtonian,* April 29, 1824.

[47] DelGaz, April 30, 1824.

[48] DelGaz, April 30, July 20, 1824; and W.T. Read, "Fire at New Castle, 1824," Oct. 13, 1864, Appendix C, Box 82B, Folder 5, HSD.

[49] *The American Farmer,* July 23, 1824.

[50] Robert Frank Brown, "Front Street, New Castle, Delaware: Architecture and Building Practices, 1687–1859" (M.A. thesis, University of Delaware, 1961), pp. 38–52.

[51] Holmes, "New Castle and Frenchtown," pp. 85–99.

[52] S. Nevins to William B. Lewis, Feb. 28, 1832, New Castle and Frenchtown Turnpike and Railroad Company Papers, HSD.

[53] Holmes, "New Castle and Frenchtown," pp. 100–12, 124–33.

[54] Holmes, "New Castle and Frenchtown," pp. 71, 118–24, 137–41.

[55] Holmes, "New Castle and Frenchtown," pp. 152–55; *Delaware State Journal* (Wilmington; hereafter DSJ), March 3, July 28, 1835; and *New Castle Gazette*, July 20, 1835.

[56] DSJ, Feb. 10, 14, 17, 21, 1837, Sept. 3, 1839; petitions to the General Assembly from citizens of Delaware, Sept. 14, 1836, citizens of Philadelphia, Feb. 7, 1837, and Dec. 24, 1838, City Council of Wilmington, 1837, Board of Trade of Wilmington, 1837, Wilmington and Susquehanna Railroad Company, 1837, Legislative Papers, DPA; Alexander B. Cooper, "The History of New Castle, Delaware From its First Settlement to the Present Time, 1651–1907," section 24, p. 3, manuscript of newspaper articles published 1907–1908, HSD; and *Laws*, 9:276–81.

[57] Holmes, "New Castle and Frenchtown," pp. 154–55; Cooper, "History of New Castle," Section 24, pp. 3–4; and *Laws*, 9:515–20.

[58] J. Snowden Bell, "The New Castle Manufacturing Company," reprinted in *Railway & Locomotive Historical Society Bulletin #18*, June 1929, pp. 28–39, originally printed in *Railway and Locomotive Engineering*, Jan. 1922; "Locomotives built at New Castle, Delaware," list compiled by Thomas Narrell, early 1950s, DPA; *Laws*, 8: 241–45; James Couper, Jr., to C.I. du Pont, May 16, June 5, 1837, June 13, 1838, C.I. du Pont Correspondence, Hagley Museum and Library; William T. Read to George Read II, Feb. 18, 1835, Richard S. Rodney Collection, HSD; DSJ, June 19, 1825; and *New Castle Gazette*, July 20, 1835.

[59] DSJ, March 27, 1840.

[60] William T. Read to George Read II, Sept. 3, 1835, Richard S. Rodney Collection, HSD; DSJ, March 11, 22, 1836; petition from citizens of the town of New Castle and others interested in the navigation of the Delaware, Jan. 1835, Legislative Papers, DPA; Gibson, ed., *Collected Essays of Richard S. Rodney*, p. 228; and U.S. Congress, House, *Harbor of New Castle*, 27th Congress, 1st Session, 1841, House Document 60, pp. 4, 7.

[61] William T. Read to George Read III, Jan. 22, 1836, George Read III to William T. Read, Jan. 22, 1836, Levi Woodbury to T. Stockton, James Booth and others, March 1, 1836, Arnold Naudain to Thomas Stockton, James

## Chapter 3 – A Town Among Cities

Booth and others, March 5, 1836, James Couper, Jr., to William T. Read, March 4, 1836, William T. Read to James Couper, Jr., March 7, 1836, "Report of a meeting of the Committee of Safety, January 3, 1837," Richard S. Rodney Collection, HSD; U.S., Congress, Senate, *Memorial of the Citizens of Newcastle, Delaware for the establishment of that place as a port of entry*, 24th Congress, 1st Session, 1836, Senate Document 58; U.S., Congress, Senate, Committee on Commerce, Report, 24th Congress, 1st Session, 1836, Senate Document 190; U.S., Congress, Senate, *Memorial of a Number of Merchants, and Others, of Philadelphia, . . .*, 25th Congress, 2d Session, 1838, Senate Document 413; U.S., Congress, *Harbor of New Castle*, 27th Congress, 1st Session, House Document 60, p. 5.

[62] DSJ, Sept. 3, 1839; Congress, *Harbor of New Castle*, p. 11.

[63] New Castle County Levy Court Minutes, March 6–15, 1827, Feb. 3–11, March 3–12, May 4–15, 1829, Feb. 2–10, March 2–13, 1830, March 5–14, 1833, Feb. 2–11, March 1–11, 1836, DPA; petitions, citizens of New Castle Hundred to the General Assembly, Dec. 1831 and Jan. 1832, Legislative Papers, DPA; and *Laws*, 8:27–29.

[64] DSJ, Feb. 14, 1832, Jan.–Feb. 1835 passim, Jan.–April 1837 passim, Feb.–June 1839 passim; "Remonstrance of Several Inhabitants of the Town of Newcastle for and in behalf of the Citizens of the Said Town, submitted to the House of Representatives of the State of Delaware, against the passage of a bill entitled, 'An act to provide for the removal of the Seat of Justice for Newcastle county, from the town of Newcastle to the city of Wilmington'," Jan. 29, 1835, Richard S. Rodney Collection, HSD; and scattered petitions and reports, 1832–1837, Legislative Papers, DPA.

[65] "Remonstrances of Several Inhabitants of the Town of Newcastle," p. 7, Richard S. Rodney Collection, HSD.

[66] *New Castle Gazette*, July 20, 1835; Common, pp. 160–62, 168, 172; DSJ, May 24, 1839.

[67] *New Castle Gazette*, July 20, 1835.

[68] William T. Read to George Read II, Feb. 18, 1835, Richard S. Rodney Collection, HSD.

[69] DSJ, June 23, 1835.

## Voices and Viewpoints

*Maria Booth Rogers of New Castle wrote to her husband James at two o'clock in the morning in the midst of the fire of April 26–27, 1824. Her eyewitness account conveys the horror of the experience, her participation in fighting the fire, her compassion for the victims, and her thankfulness that her own home and the rest of the town had been saved, and that no lives had been lost. Her unique, personal account brings to life a tragic episode in New Castle's history.*

# FIRE! 1824

*Maria Booth Rogers*

Tuesday Morning 2 oclock

My dear Husband,

We are all here in a state of alarm and confusion, a most destructive fire broke out about 3 oclock in the afternoon, in a stable or some back building of Mr. Riddle, on the wharf. The wind blowing very fresh from the north communicated to the board yard, which with all the buildings on that side of the street except the house occupied by Mr. Bowman and the two frame ones next it are all destroyed, and all on the other side from Mr. Roberts to G. Read's: with difficulty the bank and Mr. Roberts' house were saved. You can have no idea of the scene of horror it exhibited. Imagine the whole on fire extending to the other street, all the back buildings on both sides of

Water Street, the females crying, and yet very actively engaged in carrying water. I am almost exhausted with fatigue. I have been carrying water, and furniture, all the afternoon—the furniture is lying about in the streets, the market house filled, the arsenal, and almost all the street the market house stands in, some in the meeting house, and in the church yard. Mr. McCullough has lost every thing, house, store, store house, goods, furniture all destroyed, Mr. Riddle's house entirely destroyed. They sent to Wilmington for aid, and a great many came over and brought all the engines and hose, which was the means of saving Mr. Read's house, which arrested the fire on that side of the street. About twelve oclock we prepared for bed thinking the fire would not increase, as it was nearly subdued—but unfortunately the wind has changed to North East, and blowing with considerable violence, and we were again alarmed with the cry of fire together with the ringing of the bells. They are afraid of the bank catching fire. Thomas went out, but has not returned and I have concluded not to go to bed to night, for if the bank takes fire Mr. Mundally's house will go, and then if the wind should change to the south East, no human means, could save all this street. It will be a melancholy sight to you when you return to see the destruction. I shall be glad to see the day dawn, I feel so gloomy. Mama and Elizabeth went to Philadelphia this day week, so that they, and you, have escaped the dreadful scene. You will excuse all defects for I really can scarcely write. I hope I shall be able to tell you, by day light, that the fire is entirely out.

*Voices and Viewpoints*

Tuesday night.

The fire is still burning, but is has rained hard all the afternoon and no danger is now apprehended. It was really distressing this morning to walk round the town and see the desolation it has made, and those that have not where to lay their heads, except taken in by their neighbors, looking for their furniture, some in one place and some in another. However it is impossible to give you a description of the scene of distress, and yet we have reason to be thankful, that no lives were lost. If it had happened at night it would have been much worse. Altho I have not slept any except an hour or two this morning with my cloaths on, yet I feel such a dread on my mind, that I do not feel as if I wished to sleep.

I feel grateful that we have escaped, and have to feel distress only for others, at one time I was apprehensive that the whole town would be burned. When will you be at home? Write and let me know. Give my love to papa and James.

Yours affectionately
MR

There are 23 dwelling houses entirely destroyed, besides store houses, stables and other out buildings. [1]

---

[1] M.R. [Maria Rogers] to her husband [James Rogers], Tuesday morning 2 oclock [April 27, 1824], Boothhurst Collection, Historical Society of Delaware.

# Chapter Four

From the mid 1800s through the mid 1900s, manufacturing was a vital part of New Castle's economy. Writing in 1907, Alexander Cooper describes various industries in town and some of the people associated with them. This is one of Cooper's many rambling, chatty pieces on New Castle history that were published serially in the *Wilmington Sunday Star* in 1907 and 1908. The entire manuscript, "The History of New Castle, Delaware, from its First Settlement to the Present Times, 1651–1907," is in the collections of the Historical Society of Delaware. This section is reprinted with permission. Some minor editorial changes have been made.

## Manufactural Interests and Industries

*Alexander B. Cooper*

Beginning in a small way about three quarters of a century ago, New Castle has gradually developed into what may now be called a manufactural city, although some of these industries, through the financial depressions of the times, the formation of the modern trusts and from other causes, have ceased to exist. Others have come to take their places. In the 1820s there was a chair factory, where chairs of the ordinary household type were made, located in the rear, and a little to the northward of the present residence of Col. Joseph H. Rogers on the Strand. There was also a soap factory adjoining what is now his property on the northeast. The Colonel recollects them both very well but cannot now recall the names of the proprietors of either of them.[1]

The next two plants... came to New Castle, in connection with the building of the New Castle and Frenchtown Railroad in the 1830s, and consisted of the locomotive shops of that company and the New Castle Manufacturing Company. These plants, and particularly the latter, were the leaders among the pioneer locomotive works of the United States.[2] The locomotives which were constructed by the manufacturing company were especially and widely well known. The company did not prove to be a financial success; but the strength and character of its work was most excellent for those days when locomotive engineering was in its infancy.... This company built a number of engines for not only the Frenchtown road, but for other roads then being constructed and operated in other states. It built some eight or ten for the Philadelphia, Wilmington and Baltimore Road. In those days the locomotives were identified and distinguished by proper names, instead of numbers as they now are. The last one the company built for the P. W. and B. R. R. Co., the writer is informed, was the "William Penn." The company works were in the old foundry erected by it at the foot of Vine Street [now Fourth Street], and extended northwest to the foot of Union Street [now Fifth Street]....

In 1857 the late James G. Shaw, then of Chester, Pennsylvania, removed to New Castle and purchased a large tract of land to the southwest and west of the town, (including the site of the present Shawtown), which formerly belonged to Chancellor Kensey Johns, Jr. Mr. Shaw was a man of untiring energy and business enterprise. He at once took an active and leading part in the interests and development of the town. In 1860-1 he erected a large mill a little west of the present railroad station for the manufacture of cotton yarn. It was to be run and the business carried on by a manufacturing firm of Boston, Massachusetts. The civil war of 1860-5 had then fairly

## Chapter 4 – Manufactural Interests and Industries

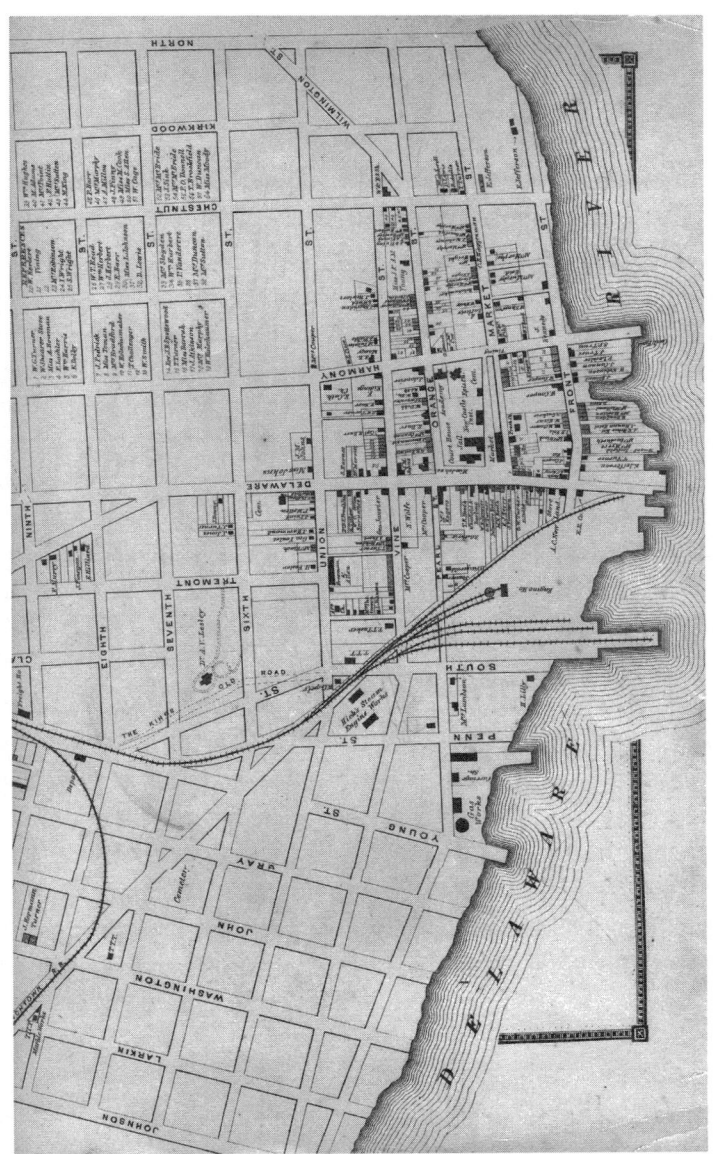

*Map of New Castle*, Atlas of the State of Delaware
*(Philadelphia: Pomeroy and Beers, 1868).*
*(Courtesy of the Historical Society of Delaware.)*

begun, with all its disturbing influences upon business and otherwise. Particularly with that branch of business in which cotton (the principle product of the South) was used. Consequently the Boston firm abandoned the contract. In 1863, Mr. Shaw having secured the necessary machinery, which had been contracted for by the Boston firm, associated himself with James G. Knowles, a man of some experience in the business, and started the mill under the name of the Triton Mills. In 1864 the great bulk of his land south of the mill was sold by him to Thomas T. Tasker of Philadelphia. In 1871 the association with Mr. Knowles was dissolved, and Mr. Shaw continued the business by himself in a successful manner until about twenty years ago. At that time mills had been erected in the Southern States—many of them on the plantations where the cotton was grown—for the manufacture of cotton yarn; so that the manufacturer of the south could sell the yarn for a less price per pound, than it would have cost to have the raw material delivered at New Castle. With this state of affairs Mr. Shaw could not compete, and the mills were closed and still remain closed.

The Triton Mills when in active operation gave employment to 150 to 200 persons, male and female, mostly residents of the town. Samuel J. Etchells, an expert in the business, was the head manager, and the yarn manufactured was of the highest grade. In July 1890, Mr. Shaw formed a corporation under the name of "The Triton Mills Company," with a view of installing new machinery and converting the mill into a manufactory of textile cotton and woolen goods. This however was not carried out further than the conveyance of the land and mills to the newly incorporated company, which was made in December 1895.

Mr. Shaw was an active and useful citizen of the town, and did much towards the advancement of its material interests. It was largely, if not entirely, through his efforts that that part of New Castle which bears his name—Shawtown—has been built up to its present dimensions; that Washington Avenue was laid out and opened, about

## Chapter 4 – Manufactural Interests and Industries

the time his mill was built; that the New Castle Water Works Company was established and water for general purposes was introduced into the town, and that gas was provided by the New Castle Gas Company for illuminating purposes, in place of the oils and fluids theretofore in use....

The New Castle Gas Company was incorporated on February 19, 1857. Howell J. Terry, James Couper, John Janvier, Peter B. Vandever, James Crippen and Thomas T. Tasker were the original corporators. The works are on the river shore in the southwesterly part of the city. The gas was first turned on and the streets lighted, amidst the cheers and jubilations of the inhabitants, on New Year's eve, December 31, 1857. Within a comparatively short time thereafter the gas was introduced into many of the private houses and public buildings of the town. The funds necessary to bring about this great and useful improvement were largely raised by private subscription to the capital stock of the company, the subscribers being actuated more by a desire to accomplish the public good than by any expectation of private gain. In order to meet the current expenses of the company, the price of gas was at first fixed at five dollars per 1,000 feet. About 30 years ago it was reduced to three dollars per 1,000 feet. It remained at this price until about fifteen years ago, and was then further reduced to the present price of one dollar and a half per 1,000 feet. Owing to the removal of the county seat to Wilmington in 1881, the jail to the workhouse at Greenbank, the subsequent introduction of electric lights for the streets by the city, and from other minor causes, the company became financially embarrassed. In 1902 the mortgage bondholders of the company sold their bonds to the Bay State Gas Company, a corporation of Delaware, whose principal place of business was in Boston, Massachusetts, and whose controlling spirit was J. Edward Addicks—a leading figure in the republican politics of the State for the last twenty years.[3] In 1903 the Bay State Gas Company became insolvent, and by proper proceedings in the courts George Wharton Pepper of Philadelphia was appointed its receiver. In calling in the assets of the company, Mr. Pepper, as such receiver and pursuant to an order of the U. S. Circuit Court of the District of Delaware, on February 27, 1904, sold the entire plant of the New Castle Gas Company to Edmund Mitchell, then and now the vice-president of the Wilmington Gas and Electric Company. Mr. Mitchell and his associates in the business at once formed a new corporation, called the New Castle Gas Light Company, which now operates the plant to the satisfaction of its patrons and with apparent success, although it has nothing to do with the lighting of the public streets. The streets are now lighted by electricity, furnished under a contract with the city, by The Delaware Water Improvement Company, who succeeded in this respect the Wilmington and New Castle Electric Railway Company. The business of the new gas company is now confined, almost exclusively, to furnishing gas to the private consumer....

About 1865, Thomas T. Tasker, of Philadelphia, having taken much interest in the affairs of New Castle, built a large brick steam

*Tasker Iron Works, 1876.*
*(Courtesy of the Historical Society of Delaware.)*

## Chapter 4 – Manufactural Interests and Industries

flour and grist mill on the southerly side of the Delaware Railroad a short distance below Washington Avenue, on a part of the land he had previously purchased from James G. Shaw. In 1872 Mr. Tasker sold this mill to the William Lea and Sons Company, who owned and operated an extensive grain and flour plant in Wilmington, on the Brandywine creek, and in conjunction with which the New Castle mill was run. The mill at New Castle was enlarged and improved in 1887, and then consisted of a large two-story brick building, 40 by 50 feet, with a two story wing, 32 by 42 feet, a one story warehouse, 35 by 70 feet, a brick engine house, 25 by 35 feet, and a grain elevator, 35 by 80 feet, with a tower of 55 feet, and of a capacity for 50,000 bushels of grain. It was an exceedingly fine plant, had a productive capacity of 350 barrels of flour per day, and employed when in full operation about 25 persons. S. Atwood Stewart was the superintendent for a number of years. Some ten years ago the mill was closed, and since then has been idle.

Thomas T. Tasker, who had built the flour mill, was largely interested as one of the owners and proprietors of the Morris-Tasker Iron Works, commonly called the Paschal Iron Works, in the southern part of Philadelphia. Indeed these works were established by him and Henry G. Morris in 1821. In 1872 he conceived the idea of removing a large part of this plant to New Castle, for the manufacture of pipes and tubes. The Morris pipe had achieved an almost world wide reputation. Accordingly, through his instrumentality and with the aid of his son, Stephen P. M. Tasker, much additional property was purchased in New Castle (including the old foundry, which was used as a moulding shop), and large brick buildings were erected during the years 1872–3 on the river, about one half of a mile southwest of the town. It held the name of the Philadelphia plant until 1876, when it was incorporated as the Delaware Iron Company, with Stephen P. M. Tasker, president; Charles Wheeler, vice-president; and T. Wister Brown, secretary and treasurer.

It does not appear to have been at first a stock company, but became so in 1886. The capital stock was $500,000, but was subsequently increased to over a million dollars. At this time (1886) M. C. McIlvaine was president; Jonathan Rowland, secretary; T. Wistar Brown, treasurer, and Lewis W. Shallcross, general manager. The principal office was in Philadelphia.

In 1883 Hiram R. Borie became the superintendent at New Castle, in the place of Joseph R. Tasker. The plant covered an area of some 35 acres of land, with a large bending mill, welding mill, finishing room and other necessary and suitable buildings thereon erected. Adjoining this property to the southwest was a large frame rolling mill, erected by Hugh M. Steel and operated by him as a supply-mill to the larger plant. This rolling mill was destroyed by fire some twenty years ago. The Delaware Iron Company when in full operation gave employment to as many as a thousand persons. In order to accommodate these people with homes convenient to their work, Richard J. Dobbins, a wealthy contractor and builder in Philadelphia, about the time the plant was started, bought the land and erected thereon from 80 to 100 small two story brick houses, adjacent to the works. This little settlement now comprises that part of New Castle called Dobbinsville [bounded by Sixth, Eighth, Clark, and Clymer Streets].

About 1899, the Delaware Iron Company associated itself with and became part of the gigantic trust or combination of pipe and tube companies known as The National Tube Company. The works at New Castle were then closed, and ceased operation entirely. During the last two or three years the plant has been gradually dismantled, by the removal of the engines, machinery, fixtures, etc. The buildings are in charge of a caretaker, and Hiram R. Borie, the general superintendent for the eastern district of The National Tube Company, is an occasional visitor in the interests of the company. Beyond this there are no signs of business life around this large and active plant of former years.

*Chapter 4 – Manufactural Interests and Industries*

NEW CASTLE OPERA HOUSE.

*New Castle Opera House, ca. early 1900s. Erected in 1879, the Opera House also served as a Masonic temple. The cupola was removed around 1950. (Courtesy of the Horace Deakyne Collection, New Castle Historical Society.)*

Another important manufacturing industry of New Castle is the large brick woolen mill now operated by the Melville Gambrill Mills Company, which was incorporated and began business in 1907. This mill was originally erected in 1873 by James G. Knowles, the former partner of James G. Shaw in the manufacture of cotton yarn. It is located at the southerly intersection of the right of way of the Delaware Railroad Company and Washington Avenue. For a short time it was run by Mr. Knowles individually, and afterwards for a number of years by the James G. Knowles Woolen Company, a corporation. Woolen fabrics were at first manufactured. The mill has been destroyed by fire a number of times, first on October 23, 1878. It was at once rebuilt and adapted to the manufacture of both woolen and cotton goods, or rather a combination of both. In 1884 it was again burned and rebuilt, and the same may be said of several subsequent occasions. In 1886, and for a few years thereafter, its business was in a most flourishing and prosperous condition. The company then employed from 200 to 250 persons. Large additions were built, new machinery put in, and what were known as "cotton worsteds," of medium grade for men's wear, were manufactured in large quantities and sold at large profits. These conditions continued for several years until adversity came, and finally in 1902 the company was declared bankrupt and its affairs wound up by the United States District Court. The real estate was the property of Mr. Knowles, individually. Consequently the next year (1903), Mr. Knowles organized a new corporation, under the name of "Fort Casimir Woolen Mills, Incorporated," and began business again. Owing to his failing health and other causes the new company did not succeed. The holders of the mortgage against the real estate foreclosed it, and the property was sold to Melville Gambrill, who now operates the plant as stated.

In walking along the roadbed of the old New Castle and Frenchtown Railroad, adjoining the Presbyterian Cemetery on the west, one may now see a row of four neat, but small two story brick

## Chapter 4 – Manufactural Interests and Industries

dwelling houses, and may desire to know their history. Some twenty-five, or perhaps a few more, years ago, Dr. Allen V. Lesley, the owner of the land, erected a large brick building for the manufacture of umbrellas. The factory was managed by Martin V. B. Buell, who had been telegraph operator for the Delaware railroad company at its New Castle station. It was run for a short time, but not proving successful was closed. Subsequently the building and ground were purchased by Israel Ridings, and the building was converted by him into the present dwellings. Mr. Ridings erected the small brick buildings, and divided into rooms the interior of the old factory.

It may be briefly mentioned in this connection that there have been several futile attempts in the last fifteen or twenty years to establish shirt factories, and at one time a factory to separate and reclaim from the sheet iron the tin on scrap tin-plate, the process for which is a modern and valuable invention. Several years ago the shirt factory experiment was tried in the Knights of Pythias hall for about six months and failed. The "tin-plate" experiment, as it was called, was also tried in the old foundry building in 1890, by a man by the name of McDevitt, but was soon abandoned.

What bids fair to be the great manufacturing industries of the city in the future, however, are the plants now in active operation, and those about to locate there. On February 21, 1903, a proposition was submitted to the Trustees of the Common, by the Brylgon Steel Casting Company of Reading, Pennsylvania, to the effect, that if the Trustees would secure for it a site, of not less than sixteen acres of land along the riverfront in the northeasterly part of the city, and pay it a cash bonus of twelve hundred dollars a year for ten years, it would remove its plant to New Castle. In order to ascertain the sentiment of the inhabitants, a town meeting was called and held on February 26 to consider the proposition. The meeting unanimously favored the proposition and formally approved it, leaving its accomplishment to the discretion of the Trustees. Afterwards, on June 28 of the same year, proper arrangements, contracts, etc., were entered into with the company. The necessary land was purchased from Francis deH. Janvier and his sister, adjoining the Glebe farm to the northeast, and in due course of time the necessary buildings, built of structural steel, were erected and the plant began operations. Speaking in a general way, its work consists in manufacturing all kinds of steel castings, by what is known as the converter or, more properly or technically speaking, the Tropenas process. When under full operation it employs about 200 persons. It is in a prosperous condition and a most valuable acquisition to the industries of the city. The president is Andrew Bryson, a popular, highly esteemed and useful citizen of the town, who is taking much interest in its local affairs, being at this writing the president of the New Castle Board of Trade. His residence is on Orange Street between Delaware and Harmony streets, in the house formerly owned by Capt. Robert H. Barr, but now belonging to George Peirce.

In the early spring of 1903, the Baldt Steel Company was incorporated under the laws of Delaware. On April 24, 1903, it entered into a contract with the Trustees of the Common. In pursuance of this contract, it bought of Francis deH. Janvier and his sister (the owners of the property) about 35 acres of land, on the riverfront, adjoining the Brylgon Company's plant on the northeast. The payment of a bonus of $6,000 was guaranteed to the Baldt Company by the Trustees, under a contract dated June 4, 1903, in annual payments of $1,000, the first payment to be made when the works were opened, and the balance, $1,000 each year thereafter, until the full sum was paid, with interest at four percent. The large buildings of steel framework and brick walls were subsequently erected and the plant began operations in 1904. The office and other buildings have since been built. When in full operation this plant is capable of giving work to at least 500 men. It manufactures steel castings of every description, by what is commonly known as the open hearth process, and can turn out castings of the largest and heaviest kind. It is also in a prosperous condition. Its president is Frederick T. Baldt, who lately

*Chapter 4 – Manufactural Interests and Industries*

resided in New Castle, in the bank building at the corner of Delaware Street and the Strand, but who now lives in Chester, Pennsylvania, from which place he came to New Castle. Mr. Baldt stands high as an expert in the steel business. He was the inventor of the Baldt anchor, now in popular use, particularly with large vessels. Individually he is a man of pleasant manners and is respected by the people of New Castle.

In order to give these plants convenient access to the public highway between New Castle and Wilmington, the trustees of

*Old Library, ca. early 1900s. Designed by William Camac of Furness, Evans & Co. of Philadelphia for the New Castle Library Company, this building on East Third Street facing the Green was completed in 1892. It is now a museum of the New Castle Historical Society. (Courtesy of the Horace Deakyne Collection, New Castle Historical Society.)*

Immanuel Church, the owners of the land, generously leased at a nominal rent sufficient ground to open two new streets, which was done by the City Council of New Castle. Sixth Street as laid down on the city map was extended into the plant of the Brylgon Company, and a few hundred feet to the northeast of Sixth Street so extended, a new street was opened and named Halliwell, which leads onto the grounds of the Baldt Company. This was done in 1904. In 1907 the Baldt Company constructed the large and handsome wharf which extends 200 yards into the river in front of its works.

Another company was incorporated in Delaware, in the latter part of 1907, by the name of the Tropenas Steel Company. This company was created by Alexandre Tropenas, a Frenchman. He stands high among the steel manufacturers of the world, and was the inventor of the Tropenas process in the manufacture of that metal. He also operates large plants in Belgium, France and England. After its incorporation, this company purchased of Seldon S. Deemer, the superintendent of the Brylgon Steel Casting Company, a large tract of land of some fifty acres, in the westerly and southwesterly part of New Castle, for the purpose of erecting a large steel plant. Surveys are now being made, gradings ascertained, etc., to carry out its purpose. The council of New Castle, in order to accommodate the company, is about to reduce the grade of Seventh Street, which passes through its lands, between Johns and Clymer streets, some seven feet below the grade heretofore established, at that point in accord with the present bed of the street, as now travelled. In aid of this plant, the Trustees of the Common have contracted to pay to Seldon S. Deemer $7,900.00 of the purchase money, in 10 years from September 1, 1907, with interest at 5 percent; provided, the plant is operated continuously for 10 years, after it starts. It must also be built and start work within two years from that date.

It may also be mentioned in this connection, that the Lukens Iron and Steel company of Coatesville, Pennsylvania, have recently purchased the Hurst and Eves farms, a little beyond the northeast-

*Chapter 4 – Manufactural Interests and Industries*

erly limits of New Castle, for the purpose of erecting another large plant. Surveys and grading have been started towards this end.

With this, is concluded the history of all the manufactural industries of New Castle, worthy of mention at this time. The writer may here express the hope, that the building of the Lukens plant, may prove to be another substantial link in a chain of industries along the riverfront, which will eventually culminate, in joining the cities of New Castle and Wilmington into one—either as a greater New Castle or a greater Wilmington.

---

[1] "Recollections of New Castle, as detailed by Joseph H Rogers, Esq., to Alexander B. Cooper… September 15th, 1905," Historical Society of Delaware (hereafter HSD), Wilmington.

[2] See J. Snowden Bell, "The New Castle Manufacturing Company," *Railway and Locomotive Engineering*, Jan. 1922, and Richard E. Hall, "The New Castle Manufacturing Company, Delaware's Pioneering Locomotive Builder" (1997), typescript, HSD.

[3] Cooper leaves much unsaid here. See John A. Munroe, *History of Delaware*, 2d ed. (Newark, Del., 1984), pp. 175–80.

## Voices and Viewpoints

# African Americans

African Americans have lived in New Castle from its earliest days. Whether enslaved or free, they struggled to live their lives in a world that placed limits and restrictions upon them. Most were servants or laborers, doing anonymous, essential, and often backbreaking work. Yet some blacks, such as Augustus Jamot in the early 1800s and Peter Jackson half a century later, had their own businesses. New Castle's African Americans also developed their own community life, most notably through Bethany Union American Methodist Episcopal Church, founded in 1815, and Mount Salem Methodist Church, founded in 1857.

Some key events in Delaware's participation in the Underground Railroad took place in New Castle. In December 1845 Samuel Hawkins, a free black, helped his wife and six children, all of whom were slaves, escape to freedom from Maryland. John Hunn of Middletown and Thomas Garrett of Wilmington assisted them. During their journey, the family spent some time in the New Castle County Jail while Garrett obtained a ruling from Judge James Booth that allowed them to continue their journey to freedom. For this, the two owners of Mrs. Hawkins and the children sued Garrett and Hunn in federal court. The trial took place in New Castle in May 1848. Both men were found guilty and punished with fines and damages. Garrett addressed the court after his trial, and had his speech printed in the *Blue Hen's Chicken*, an antislavery newspaper.[1]

## Augustus Jamot

*The only information about race comes from George Read's notation on the back of this letter of introduction that Jamot was a "mulatto French barber." Jamot moved to New Castle and opened a hairdressing shop where he also sold feathers, beads, and related goods.*

Sir,

The Bearer Augustus Jamot is about to visit New Castle with a view to the establishing himself there as a Hair dresser. He has been known to me these Ten years past, & I have no hesitation in recommending him as a very *sober, honest obliging* good tempered man. He lived in my family 18 months & conducted himself generally to my satisfaction. We parted at his own request.

He dresses & shaves tolerably well & plays on the violin & and is an excellent waiter.

I take the liberty of giving you this character of the man that he may be known in case it should be necessary to refer for character &c.

I am respectfully
Yr obt...
Geo Harrison
Phila April 19th 1803

Geo Read Esquire
New Castle[2]

*Voices and Viewpoints*

*Bethany UAME Church, Fifth and Williams Streets, 1930s–1940s. (Courtesy of the Historical Society of Delaware.)*

## Peter Jackson

*In 1907, Alexander Cooper wrote about Peter Jackson, who ran a popular oyster restaurant in the 1850s:*

Peter Jackson, a prominent and intelligent colored man[sic], who more than fifty years ago was the sexton of Immanuel Church, kept an oyster saloon in an old brick house which stood on the southwest side of Delaware street, in the rear of the old Mansfield house, (at the corner of that street and Front Street,) upon the site of the present frame dwelling. Peter was a popular and accommodating restaurateur. Nothing pleased him better than to see his customers pleased—among whom he reckoned the best men of the town.[3]

*Mount Salem Methodist Church, 140 East Fourth Street, 1930s–1940s. (Courtesy of the Historical Society of Delaware.)*

## Thomas Garrett

*Excerpt from Thomas Garrett's speech at the close of his trial in 1848:*

I should have done violence to my convictions of duty, had I not made use of all the lawful means in my power to liberate those people, and assist them to become men and women, rather than leave them in the condition of chattels personal. I am called an Abolitionist, once a name of reproach, but one I have ever been proud to be considered worthy of being called. For the last twenty-five years I have been engaged in the cause of this despised and injured race, and consider their cause worth suffering for; but owing to the multiplicity of other engagements, I could not devote so much of my time and mind to their cause as I otherwise should have done. The impositions and persecutions practiced on those unoffending and innocent brethren, are extreme beyond endurance. I am now placed in a situation in which I have not so much to claim my attention as formerly, and I now pledge myself, in the presence of this assembly, to use all lawful and honorable means to lessen the burdens of this oppressed people, and endeavor according to ability furnished to burst their chains asunder, and set them free—not relaxing my efforts on their behalf while blessed with health, and a slave remains to tread the soil of the state of my adoption—Delaware; and after mature reflection, I can assure this assembly it is my opinion at this time that the verdicts you have given the prosecutors against John Hunn and myself, within the past few days, will have a tendency to raise a spirit of inquiry throughout the length and breadth of the land, respecting this monster evil (slavery), in many minds that has not heretofore investigated the subject. The reports of those trials will be published by editors from Maine to Texas and the Far West; and what must be the effect produced? It will no doubt add hundreds, perhaps thousands, to the present large and rapidly increasing army of abolitionists. The injury is great to us who are the immediate sufferers by your verdict, but I believe the verdicts you have given us within the last few days will have a powerful effect in bringing about the abolition of slavery in this country, this land of boasted freedom, where not only the slave is fettered at the south by his lordly master, but the white man at the north is bound as in chains to do the bidding of his southern masters.[4]

[1] For more information, see James A. McGowan, *Station Master on the Underground Railroad, the Life and Letters of Thomas Garrett* (Moylan, Penn., 1977).

[2] Geo. Harrison to Geo. Read, April 19, 1803, Richard S. Rodney Collection, Historical Society of Delaware. Jamot advertised in the *Mirror of the Times* (Wilmington) on April 21 and December 15, 1804.

[3] Alexander B. Cooper, "The History of New Castle, Delaware, from Its First Settlement to the Present Time, 1651–1907" (manuscript of newspaper articles published in 1907–1908), part 40, page 4, Historical Society of Delaware.

[4] *Blue Hen's Chicken*, June 9, 1848.

# Chapter Five

During the first half of the twentieth century, New Castle was a quiet town whose people lived in buildings and streets that had served their predecessors for generations. Historic structures housed stores and businesses that met the needs of everyday life. The text of this section, "New Castle Today," comes from the first edition of *New Castle on the Delaware*, written by the Delaware Federal Writers' Project and published by the New Castle Historical Society in 1936, and is reprinted with permission. The photographs recall a variety of New Castle scenes from 1900 to the early 1950s.

# New Castle Memories, 1900–1950

## *"New Castle Today," 1936*

Lying close to the Delaware River, barely twenty feet above sea level, the old town of New Castle is now the center of the corporate community (population 4,131). The town's enchantment is compounded of seemliness and taste, of completeness and a sense of authentic continuity with the past without loss of its living and livable quality. The broad Green—where ancient elms and a level sward of grass set off in fine proportion some mellow examples of the builders' art—and the few streets of old houses immediately beyond the edges of the Green form a whole that can be comprehended almost at a glance. Yet this whole provides so extensive and spacious a range of interest that its effect is to widen mental and physical horizons, not to narrow them. Like the pages of an absorbing book, the streets are filled with the record and the materials of history, adventure, romance; of political, economic and social drama, all in a language human and simple, yet dignified and impressive.

These streets extend from the Strand by the water's edge to Sixth Street on the west, and from Chestnut to Harmony and to Delaware Streets north and south.

Conformity to the regular plan of the streets by all the houses and buildings, except for Immanuel Church on the corner of the Green, contributes here to a pleasant order and design suggesting intelligent purpose rather than formality. The purpose, indicating a certainty of the importance of environment and man's relation to it, goes back to Peter Stuyvesant, governor of the Dutch possessions in America in the middle of the seventeenth century. It was he who laid out the streets and the Green behind the original fort from which the town started, and set aside some common land for wood and pasture.

The fort was built upon Sand Hook extending out into the river from the end of present Chestnut Street, a point of land long ago washed away, its location now indicated by a marker near the slip of the New Castle-Pennsville-New Jersey ferry.

Most of the early Dutch houses and the log homes of Swedes and Finns have been replaced by eighteenth century buildings and by some of the early nineteenth century, appropriate to the Colonial capital and early capital of the State; for New Castle held both honors and was the county seat for over two hundred years, until this function was surrendered to Wilmington, up the river, little more than fifty years ago. Of the buildings which stood here in the old town during the main colonial period and early statehood of Delaware, all but a few are here today. Time and an element of timelessness in the work of the builders leave only the flavor without the urgency of the days and lives of the early citizens. But though change in the currents of history has eliminated tension and stir from the local life, it is a refreshing serenity that remains.

Beneath more than a score of roofs within this ancient neighborhood is work so lovingly designed and skillfully executed that it

*Chapter 5 – New Castle Memories*

draws the discriminating among architects, and charms every person who has a taste for the art of building. Progress has accomplished enough to make the old town agreeable and congenial to its inhabitants, but has left unspoiled what men wrought in the golden age of wood and brick.

The spirit of the town is not that of an antiquarian society at all. The dwellers are as preoccupied with their own affairs as are Americans elsewhere. They take the town as a matter of course, a part of the background of their days, and like it as it is. Old Delaware

*George B. Tobin & Sons Meat Market, ca. 1930s.*
*(Courtesy of the Historical Society of Delaware.)*

Street, the main thoroughfare, is the chief business and shopping center; and shops here and elsewhere display not merely antiques but an ample variety of the ordinary things of present need. Automobiles make their way about, avoiding mostly those streets on which the cobblestone pavements of 1815 have been allowed to remain.

Rows of plain old-fashioned houses—and here and there a single house—in some of the streets beyond those in the close environment of Strand and Green have a simplicity and dignity wholly in keeping with the qualities of the central town.

Delaware Street, beyond Fourth, soon runs into a section of modern dwellings, for the most part little different in character from those of any average town of four thousand people in the Middle States of the Atlantic seaboard. This section occupies cross streets on both sides of Delaware Street. Along the river, south of Delaware Street, lies a tract of level vacant land called the Battery, casually used as a recreation field.

At Ninth and South Streets, close to the railroad station, is an outlying section of small dwellings known as Shawtown. Another separate section, near the western corner of the town limits adjoining Bellanca airplane field, bears the name of Washington Park. Several settlements of colored [sic] people lie within a few blocks of Delaware Street, north and south. Quite separate and to the northeast, but still within the municipal limits, is a modern medium-income residential section known as Baldton; otherwise the territory northeast of Chestnut Street is chiefly open land.

The town limits, which form an irregular oblong, about half as wide as long, much outrun the main built-up areas and extend for two miles along the Delaware shore. The width of the town's territory inland from the river averages about a mile. Most of the inhabitants live near the river within a half square mile, at the center of this tract.

The territory immediately outside of the city is still largely agricultural; near the river much of it is too low for cultivation, but at a

## Chapter 5 – New Castle Memories

short distance to the north and west the surface rises in gentle slopes to elevations of 60 feet or more. The country is open and bears excellent yields of wheat and corn. Here and there on the higher lands near the town, the horizon is varied by small but well-grown tracts of woodland.

Industrial establishments have not become lodged in the heart of New Castle. Some are down stream between the railroad and the river front, some up stream, and one—that of the Bellanca Aircraft Corporation—is inland at the southwestern edge of the town.

Among the great majority of citizens regularly employed, there is no sharp distinction in regard to occupations between the natives and the people of recently Americanized stock. Employment in the local manufacturing plants provides the most general form of livelihood. A comparatively small group is employed in Wilmington, which is near enough to make the daily trip an easy matter. Some residents of Italian origin are trained workers in the manufacture of

*Looking up the Strand from Harmony Street, September 20, 1930.*
*(Courtesy of the Historical Society of Delaware.)*

airplanes. The Negro group includes not only ordinary laborers, farm help and household workers, but a fair portion of men regularly employed in neighboring steel plants.

In point of numbers the native whites of early American descent appear to make up about half of the population. Of the other half, persons of Irish nativity or origin, next in number, constitute about 900; Negroes are estimated at 700; there is a small Polish group, possibly 50, and several families of Jews.

The Irish group, chiefly associated with the Roman Catholic parish (established 1807), has grown with the town; St. Peter's Roman Catholic Church, at 5th and Harmony Streets, now includes Italian and Polish as well as Irish and American communicants.

Because from earliest times New Castle was a court town, and the meeting place of the Colonial Assembly (1704–1777), also a county seat until 1881, it was the place of residence of lawyers, judges and county officers and of men prominent in State and national affairs. A small group of members of these families historically associated with the town, who continue to live there, exercises an important influence by reason of traditional connection with local affairs. Some members of this group hold public office and most of them are active in the movement to protect significant historic survivals, including the ancient architectural beauties of the town. A few Delawareans of means, not related to the town's early inhabitants, have made New Castle their residence as a matter of personal selection.

The distinction of New Castle today is due to the busy daily life that has gone on in it without break through the centuries, achieving a fairly congenial blending of old and new in activity and interests. This is something rather rare in our country, rarer than in parts of Europe where a town normally has not only length, breadth and height, but also an imposing time dimension accepted as one of the realities of the place.

## Chapter 5 – New Castle Memories

*The New Castle waterfront, late 1800s–early 1900s.
The long pier is at the end of Delaware Street.
(Courtesy of the Horace Deakyne Collection, New Castle Historical Society.)*

*Shad skiffs at the Delaware Street wharf, late 1800s–early 1900s.
New Castle fishermen caught huge quantities of shad, a favorite
springtime delicacy, during the late 1800s and early 1900s.
Overfishing and pollution ended the harvest.
(Courtesy of the Horace Deakyne Collection, New Castle Historical Society.)*

350 Years of New Castle, Delaware

Two views of Delaware Street opposite the Courthouse. Above, early 1900s (Courtesy of the Historical Society of Delaware); below, 1940s (Courtesy of the Horace Deakyne Collection, New Castle Historical Society). The building with the archway (just behind the big awning) in the older view has been transformed into the Acme Market in the newer photograph. Today, that building is the Wilmington Trust Bank.

*Chapter 5 – New Castle Memories*

*Two views of the drugstore at Second and Delaware Streets. Above, ca. 1930s (Courtesy of the Historical Society of Delaware); below, September 27, 1952 (Courtesy of the Horace Deakyne Collection, New Castle Historical Society).*

*Number 3 School, which became St. Anthony's Club, no date.
New Castle's Italian community began in the late 1800s and early 1900s.
A group of men formed the St. Anthony's Club in the early 1930s. In 1933
they bought the old Number 3 School, which they remodeled into a clubhouse.
The club provided a place for men to gather for recreation and community
activities. St. Anthony's Club sponsored Americanization classes and sports
teams. The club is still part of New Castle's community life.
(Courtesy of the Horace Deakyne Collection, New Castle Historical Society.)*

*Chapter 5 – New Castle Memories*

Hotel Louise, 226–228 Delaware Street, ca. 1930s. Originally a residence, this building has long served as a hotel, inn, or tavern.
(Courtesy of the Historical Society of Delaware.)

Interior of the Courthouse Tea Room, no date. The tea room was a popular restaurant for many years.
(Courtesy of the Horace Deakyne Collection, New Castle Historical Society.)

*Delaware Street looking west from Third Street, ca. 1915. The trolley provided convenient transportation to Wilmington. (Courtesy of the Historical Society of Delaware.)*

*New Castle Institute, January 5, 1930. The Arsenal, built by the federal government in 1809, housed a school from 1852 until 1930. High school students are lined up outside. (Courtesy of the Historical Society of Delaware.)*

*Chapter 5 – New Castle Memories*

*Above, looking down West Fifth Street from South Street, ca. 1930s; below, the Good Will Fire Company on South Street, looking towards West Fifth Street, ca. 1930s.*
*(Both courtesy of the Historical Society of Delaware.)*

*Platt grocery store, Second and Delaware streets, ca. 1950. The store, founded by Edward V. Platt, was in business from 1902 until 1960. Oscar Devenish is the man in the white apron. (Courtesy of the Horace Deakyne Collection, New Castle Historical Society.)*

*Chapter 5 – New Castle Memories*

*Entrance to the New Castle-Pennsville Ferries, foot of Chestnut Street, ca. 1940s. Until the first span of the Delaware Memorial Bridge opened in August 1951, the ferry offered the easiest way to travel to New Jersey from northern Delaware.*
*(Courtesy of the Horace Deakyne Collection, New Castle Historical Society.)*

## Voices and Viewpoints

*In the early 1900s, New Castle residents and others began to become aware of the need to preserve their town's heritage. In 1920, a Wilmington newspaper published a lengthy editorial on the need to preserve the Read House. Progress was slow, however, and the Great Depression and World War II did not help. In the late 1940s, a study researched and evaluated New Castle's unique resources and appealed to the town to preserve and protect its historic assets.*

# Preserving a Treasure Town

*Excerpt from "Buy the Read Mansion," 1920*

The recent transfer in the ownership of the old Read house in New Castle, that has been unoccupied since the death of its former owner several months ago, creates some concern lest the property be eventually disposed of, torn down or stripped of its splendid interior fittings. It is stated that there has been as much bid for the woodwork of the building as the entire property would bring if it were conditioned that the fittings be left undisturbed. In other words, the carved wood fittings, the wonderful doors and windows and stair railings would sell for more than the whole property intact.

It would be a grave crime to let the old house come into inappreciative ownership and to think of its being gutted of its treasures makes one shudder. We have no knowledge that such is intended, but Every Evening feels, with almost every citizen of the State, that the old house on the New Castle Strand should be under some sort of public control or ownership so that it would never be demolished nor dismantled.

It has a history that dates back to the beginning of things in Delaware; it cradled some of the ablest men who went from Delaware to contribute big parts in the formation of the government in its most trying days; it was built with a superb elegance that has never been surpassed in the more than a century of construction since; it stands with the strength of Gibraltar today almost untouched by the blight of time....

It perhaps might be purchased by the State, or by some of our societies, and put to some use that would more than warrant the expenditure for purchase and upkeep. For example it might be utilized as a permanent show place of colonial relics of Delaware, a museum illustrating a period of the State's history when despite her small area she contributed the ablest men and best thought to the founding and upbuilding of the nation. There are possibly enough men and women of means in Delaware interested in preserving this superb old pile to promptly take care of the purchase price, and the cost of maintenance could be easily met. As a museum it would attract visitors from all parts of the country and would add greatly to the outside world's knowledge of the Diamond State.[1]

*Voices and Viewpoints*

## Excerpts from "New Castle, Delaware: A Report Concerning Its History & Future," 1949

Beside the broad Delaware River, in the state of Delaware, is a distinguished and charming bit of early-American civilization. Here in old New Castle are streets and structures, compact and complete, a unique embodiment of our cherished past unequalled elsewhere. Yet with all its history, all its mellow brick and worn cobble, cupola and spire, graceful doorway and burnished knocker, it is of the present in full measure, livable and lived in ....

The study of New Castle, Delaware was begun in November 1946, underwritten by Daniel Moore Bates and Louise du Pont Crowninshield. These sponsors, inspired by the inherent beauty of the town, its unique architectural qualities and its rich historic background of almost three centuries, are also deeply conscious that time cannot be relied upon to continue its kind treatment. They recognized that accompanying the approach of needed new housing and industrial expansion a very definite effort must be made to prevent destroying the character of the town center of old New Castle....

Throughout the work of this survey, the authors of the report have experienced a growing conviction toward the principle of preservation rather than restoration. They are concerned to make an urgent plea to the citizenry of New Castle to hold on to what they already possess.

Carefully considered zoning regulations, affecting the central town before it is too late, will protect this heritage. These streets and buildings and gardens which speak so eloquently of the past, are in no way outmoded in their present usage and are in every way worthy of a much longer life.[2]

## 350 Years of New Castle, Delaware

[1] *Wilmington Every Evening,* June 23, 1920.
[2] Brochure, New Castle Restoration Papers, Historical Society of Delaware.

# Chapter Six

Modern New Castle consists of a quiet historic core surrounded by a spread-out area of modern businesses and residences. For more than fifty years, historic preservation has been a major theme in the central area. This article tells how New Castle developed its commitment to historic preservation within a living community. It was first published in *Delaware History* 25 (1992–93): 77–105 and is reprinted with permission.

## "The Gospel of New Castle": Historic Preservation in a Delaware Town

*Deborah Van Riper Harper*

Although Delawareans know New Castle as the colonial capital of their state, and hundreds of schoolchildren visit it annually when studying state history, out-of-staters must usually make a deliberate effort to discover the town. It is not a place that anyone would know from simply passing through because the roads do not pass through it; they only pass it by. Over the centuries New Castle has repeatedly suffered the fate of being passed by. At various times a seat of government, manufacturing, and transportation, it has always been eclipsed by other cities so that today the mayor worries that the town has become a "bedroom community" with no economic base of its own.[1]

One business does prosper in New Castle, though, and that is tourism. When the town lost its preeminence in transportation and trading in the first half of the nineteenth century, it fell into an economic slump that prevented many residents from dramatically changing their homes, so that it retained the appearance of its Federal-era heyday. Visitors today stroll down cobblestone streets past antique shops and historic houses, or wander along the path that follows the river in Battery Park, imagining the merchant ships that docked at the wharf in days long past. The town's romantic image is enhanced by the program of historic preservation that has been followed in New Castle for so long and to such an extent that one early supporter has referred to it as "the gospel of New Castle."[2]

The origins of America's historic preservation movement are found in the mid nineteenth century. As the United States gradually rose from an insecure fledgling nation to a world power, Americans began to take pride in their accomplishments, which resulted in a new appreciation for the people and events that had brought them such success. This included the veneration of places that had witnessed American triumphs. Charles B. Hosmer, Jr., has noted that even before the Civil War one finds "abundant evidence of an emergent national consciousness that caused some individuals to look upon the preservation of historic sites as a sign of cultural maturity."[3]

Early activists cited a structure's antiquity and its association with hallowed persons or events as justification for its preservation. The strongest rallying cry sounded when a building bore an association with George Washington. His godlike stature encouraged Ann Pamela Cunningham's successful drive in the 1850s to preserve Mount Vernon as a national shrine. Her effort was the first attempt to establish a national base of support for historic preservation. Other early campaigns were not as well organized, and many failed; but the demolition of an important structure, such as the John Hancock Mansion in Boston, motivated preservationists to prevent additional losses.

## Chapter 6 – Historic Preservation in a Delaware Town

In the late nineteenth and early twentieth centuries, a rising sense of national consciousness encouraged widespread enthusiasm for historic preservation as a vehicle for instilling American values in the vast numbers of immigrants who arrived here. Many "established" Americans, whose ancestors had arrived generations earlier, feared that their traditions would be undermined by the influx of foreign ideas. Anticipating the very destruction of their way of life, they attempted to indoctrinate the newcomers with their own ideals. Part of the process of Americanization included visits to sites so steeped in history that the foreigners would come to value American traditions above their own.[4] Eventually, disillusioned by their experience with global involvement in World War I, Americans became so isolationist in their outlook that legislation was passed in 1924 that severely restricted immigration to the United States.

The next decade saw the establishment of many shrines to American democracy. In 1924 the American Wing opened at the Metropolitan Museum of Art in New York City, followed shortly thereafter by Henry Ford's Greenfield Village in Dearborn, Michigan, and John D. Rockefeller's Colonial Williamsburg. Those museums sought not only to educate immigrants, but also to glorify American achievement for the edification of all people. Many took advantage of the freedom provided by higher wages, increased leisure time, and the newly popular automobile to travel to national parks and historic sites.[5]

In addition to greater freedom, the mobility provided by inexpensive cars also brought problems. People took jobs far away from their hometowns, which resulted in the loss of extended family networks and a related concern for the breakdown of traditional values. In addition, the many new highways, filling stations, parking lots and repair shops intruded upon bucolic farmlands and forests.[6] Preservation was seen not only as the glorification of American achievement but also as a way to hold on to a landscape, as well as a way of life, that was changing much too fast.

The course of preservation in New Castle parallels the national movement. Its stirrings are evident even in the early 1820s, when John Watson, passing through the town, described the humility he felt at the sight of the ancient Tile House on the Strand.[7] He noted the irons proclaiming the date "1687" imbedded in the front of the structure, a date which provided the house with an aura of timeworn nobility.

After its demolition in 1884, the Tile House assumed legendary status in the minds of town residents. The building inspired local artists whose images of the house were more or less fanciful, but consistent in the prominent display of the date irons. In fact, the date of the building's erection is conjectural, and the date irons may not have been original to it. All that has been ascertained regarding the date of construction is that the building did not exist when John Boyer bought the property in 1678, but after his death around 1704 his daughters' inheritance included a substantial brick house on the plot. The irons are not present in Benjamin Latrobe's depiction of the Tile House on his 1804–05 survey of New Castle; since his view does include other significant details, it is unlikely that he simply ignored them. The house was renovated in the early nineteenth century and it is possible that the irons were added then, but if so, that fact was forgotten by 1884.[8] By that time, the 1687 date was considered accurate, and the Tile House came to be viewed as New Castle's John Hancock Mansion—a terrible loss, one not to be repeated .

One person interested in the lost Tile House was local artist Laussat Richter Rogers. Like others, he painted images of the old landmark, but his influence in New Castle went beyond painting. He carried out several restorations in New Castle in the early twentieth century, including those of the Amstel House and Immanuel Episcopal Church.[9]

The Amstel House, so named by the owners for whom Rogers did his restoration, was home to such prominent early Delawareans as Nicholas Van Dyke, acting president of Delaware between 1783

## Chapter 6 – Historic Preservation in a Delaware Town

and 1786, and his son-in-law Kensey Johns, who served as state chancellor. Had Van Dyke and Johns not been famous in their own right, their place in history, along with that of the Amstel House, would nevertheless have been assured by the legend that George Washington visited the house for the wedding of Johns to Van Dyke's daughter Ann in 1784. The house changed hands several times in the decades following, ultimately suffering the indignity of having its spaces divided up after 1870 for use by various tenants. Such destruction, however, was not sufficient to blot the vision of Washington's presence, so when the house was purchased by Rogers's relatives Sophia and Henry Hanby Hay, they commissioned him to restore its former splendor. The grandeur to which Rogers restored the house possibly exceeded its original stature, for he is believed to have added architectural elements to create an ideal colonial relic.[10]

Rogers's changes to Immanuel Church were part of a long series of renovations that began soon after the church was built in the early 1700s. It was enlarged several times in the eighteenth century, but the nineteenth century saw the most dramatic changes. In the 1820s William Strickland, formerly assistant to Benjamin Latrobe but by then one of the leading architects of the day, added the transepts and tower with its spire. Thereafter the church's exterior experienced few alterations, but its interior reflected changing tastes. In the 1850s, the sanctuary was Victorianized with the chancel recessed into the tower and a permanent altar installed against the backdrop of a large stained glass window, the whole crowned by an overarching gilt inscription, "The Lord is in His Holy Temple." By the early twentieth century, the backlash against the excesses of Victorian taste demanded the elimination of those influences from a half century earlier. Rogers, a member of the church, was enlisted to make the changes.

In the early 1900s Rogers began "correcting" the Victorian Immanuel by introducing architectural details in the colonial revival style. He designed a new pulpit, altar, and lectern, and in 1918 he replaced the stained glass window.[11] The *Wilmington Every Evening* greeting his efforts with accolades, described the earlier window as "a monstrosity" and Rogers's improvements as "rightly named, and not the kind that will make the heads of future generations hang in shame, because their forebearers had bad taste instead of good."[12]

Rogers also played a part in the restoration of the George Read II House in the 1920s for its new owners, Philip and Lydia Laird. Both of the Lairds came from prominent Maryland families, but they met and married in Wilmington, where Philip was a partner in his brother's firm, Laird and Co. They acquired the Read House in 1920, and in 1925 Rogers was asked to create a rustic taproom in the basement of the house. A casual counterpart to the formal rooms upstairs, the space epitomized how freely early collectors brought together a hodgepodge of old artifacts to create an ideal colonial fantasy.[13]

Already a well-known property before the Lairds came to New Castle, the Read House fostered a sense of pride among townspeople. Built between 1797 and 1804 by George Read II, son of a signer of the Declaration of Independence and the United States Constitution, it was considered pretentious when new, but by the early twentieth century its grandeur and patriotic associations endeared it to town residents. When the Lairds first saw the house in 1920 it was for sale, to the dismay of the local people. An editorial in the *Wilmington Every Evening* voiced the concerns of all those who knew the house:

> It would be a grave crime to let the old house come into inappreciative ownership and to think of its being gutted of its treasures makes one shudder… [the] Every Evening feels, with most every citizen of the state, that the old house on the New Castle Strand should be under some sort of public control or ownership so that it would never be demolished nor dismantled.[14]

The Lairds' purchase of the Read House provided the means of achieving the editorialist's goal. They immediately set about restor-

*Chapter 6 – Historic Preservation in a Delaware Town*

*New Castle Presbyterian Church, early 1900s. This postcard shows the congregation's two church buildings. (Courtesy of the Historical Society of Delaware.)*

ing the House, although their "restoration" incorporated many changes to the building. They did not attempt to determine exactly how the structure had looked in George Read's day, nor to re-create his taste, but neither did they violate his intent. In fact, they did exactly what George Read had done one hundred years previously: they used their home to illustrate the epitome of fashion and good taste according to prevailing standards. Ultimately, through the Lairds' generosity, the Read House did become a museum open to the public, but that was decades in the future, and after the Lairds' influence on preservation in New Castle had moved beyond the sidewalks of the Strand.[15]

The Read House first opened informally to the public in May 1924 as a featured attraction in the first "Day in Old New Castle." Still held every year, "A Day in Old New Castle" was organized by Anne Rodney Janvier, a descendant of George Read, as a fund-raiser for Immanuel Church. The first organized promotion of New Castle's historic treasures, the day provided a chance for the public to visit the old houses and sip tea served by hostesses in period costume. "If you're especially lucky," one writer tempted, "you may find yourself drinking a julep in a garden under lavender-blossomed paulownia trees."[16] Beyond this, the day also supplied New Castle's response to the Met's American Wing and the Immigration Act of 1924. Already possessing a substantial immigrant population in its West End, the town now had a way to instill proper American values into the foreigners residing so close to the colonial stronghold. The churches, the Court House, and the Old Town Hall reminded the public of the moral wisdom upon which the nation was founded, while the stately houses conveyed the quiet strength of home and hearth.

The Lairds' participation in "A Day in Old New Castle" led to their involvement in other preservation efforts in the town. In March 1929 the Amstel House, having changed hands after the Hanbys' restoration, was to be sold. Concerned that it would be altered or demolished, Philip Laird and other prominent townsfolk advocated the formation of a corporation to purchase the property. Touting the names of Nicholas Van Dyke, Kensey Johns, and George Washington, the group sought funds to preserve the house as a "model home of the Colonial period."[17] By December 1931, with the property purchased and free of debt, Laird, Richard S. Rodney, C. Douglass Buck, and Francis Janvier sought to establish a non-stock corporation to provide for the care of the building.[18] They advocated a self-perpetuating board of trustees, to ensure that "the building would always be in charge of those most interested in its preservation and welfare." They also recommended purchasing the adjoining lot, originally part of the Amstel House property, in order to remove a building that they perceived to be a fire hazard. At a meeting held on December 19, the attendees voted to incorporate the New Castle Society for the Preservation of Antiquities, which would be reincorporated in 1934 as the New Castle Historical Society. Among those elected to the board of directors was Philip Laird.[19]

## Chapter 6 – Historic Preservation in a Delaware Town

While the New Castle Historical Society pursued its mission to preserve the Amstel House, another group organized with the intent of preserving all of New Castle. The Delaware Society for the Preservation of Antiquities was founded in January 1937 with Mary Wilson Thompson as president. Prior to accepting her office, Thompson urged the leadership role upon another of the society's members, Col. Daniel Moore Bates. He declined the offer, claiming to be too busy in other enterprises to give the position the attention it deserved. He assured her, though, of his deep interest in the society, stating that Delaware provided a wonderful opportunity for such an endeavor, especially in the old town of New Castle.[20]

Bates was a native Delawarean, born in Wilmington in the year of the nation's centennial, 1876. Educated in private schools in Wilmington and Philadelphia and a graduate of the Massachusetts Institute of Technology, he began his career in the textile industry with Joseph Bancroft & Sons Co. in Wilmington. He spent his working years with several textile and engineering firms and developed a strong interest in scientific management. During World War I, he served as a major and colonel in the ordnance department of the United States Army. In World War II, he spent two and one-half years teaching mathematics to servicemen at the University of Delaware. Bates did not own property in New Castle, but lived northwest of Wilmington in Centreville where his neighbors included Henry Francis du Pont and Louise du Pont Crowninshield, both of whom demonstrated great interest in preserving relics of the American past, and both of whom Bates counted as friends. It may have been their influence that encouraged him to pursue the possibilities of preservation in New Castle, which he viewed initially as an outlet for his creative energies as he retired from active business. So although he referred to New Castle casually as an area where the new Delaware Society for the Preservation of Antiquities might find opportunity, his interest in the town was hardly casual.[21]

Bates's interest in New Castle extended at least as far back as 1933, when, as a member of the Society of Colonial Wars in the State of Delaware, he received a communiqué from Electus D. Litchfield of the Society in the State of New York regarding the future of New Castle. The Society of Colonial Wars, an hereditary fraternity organized in 1892 to honor the memory of colonials who served in the military, included as part of its mission the preservation of historic sites. Litchfield had visited New Castle and believed the town could benefit from the society's influence. He encouraged Bates to work to have New Castle declared an historic monument and placed under the care of the Society of Colonial Wars in the State of Delaware. He also suggested that while the state of Delaware itself need not purchase any property in the town, an arrangement might be worked

*Aerial view of the Strand, ca. 1940s, showing the George Read II House and Gardens. (Courtesy of the Historical Society of Delaware.)*

## Chapter 6 – Historic Preservation in a Delaware Town

out whereby property owners would maintain their homes in original condition and occasionally open them to the public in exchange for exemption from taxation.[22]

Bates took Litchfield's suggestions seriously and decided to pursue the possibility of seeing New Castle restored in the same manner as Williamsburg. In 1934 he wrote to the Reverend W. A. R. Goodwin, the Virginia clergyman who had captured Rockefeller's interest for Williamsburg, to inform him of the possibilities of New Castle. Goodwin wrote back at length. Already personally familiar with New Castle, he shared Bates's enthusiasm for its potential, but raised an issue that was to plague all of Bates's efforts: New Castle had no Rockefeller. The problems that Bates faced were different from those encountered in Williamsburg, where financial needs were supplied by one individual and the involvement of state and local agencies was limited. Goodwin stressed the need for concerted action and a strong national program for preservation to assist individuals and community groups, something not yet available to assist the New Castle effort.[23]

Bates hoped that the newly formed Delaware Society for the Preservation of Antiquities would provide a pool of resources to help him fulfill his goal. He was, however, cautious in his approach, recognizing that potential supporters might be scared off by the difficulties they would come up against. One of the early meetings of the society, in the spring of 1937, featured Litchfield and Goodwin as speakers, their presence arranged by Bates. For the same meeting, he also invited his old friend and schoolmate Andrew Hepburn to make a presentation. Hepburn was a partner in the Boston architectural firm of Perry, Shaw, and Hepburn, which had carried out the restoration of Colonial Williamsburg. Bates was candid in his invitation to Hepburn to speak at the society's May gathering:

> The meeting Friday we want to devote to the subject of the work done at Williamsburg... without laying too much stress upon New Castle... There are some people

among the older residents there who are very shy about committing themselves in any way to any sort of outside regulation, or zoning restrictions, etc., and we do not want to try to shape up any New Castle program until interest generally in these matters has been aroused, and until the possible leaders in Delaware in such a movement can have the benefit of consultation and advice from yourself and Dr. Goodwin and Mr. Litchfield.[24]

After the May meeting, Electus Litchfield wrote to Mary Thompson recommending the immediate organization of a foundation that would strive to preserve New Castle in perpetuity. The first priority of this foundation would be to sponsor a survey of the town to determine which of the buildings should be designated historic monuments. Among those he recommended for a seat on the committee were Philip Laird and Daniel Moore Bates.[25]

The Delaware Society for the Preservation of Antiquities prepared to take on that role of preserving New Castle through its efforts to preserve the so-called Old Dutch House on Third Street. Bates wrote to W. A. R. Goodwin in July 1937 that the society stood a good chance of obtaining at least the control of, and possibly the title to, that ancient building; by December, the society owned the house. Five members of the society—H. Rodney Sharp, Alfred Bissell, Mrs. William C. Spruance, Mrs. Macmillan Hoopes, and Bates—underwrote the purchase cost of $2,500. In a letter sent to members of the finance committee announcing the purchase of the house, committee chairman Bates reported that an additional $7,500 would be needed to renew the building's understructure and foundation, which had suffered from termites. Beyond the money required to restore the building's structural integrity, still more would have to be raised to furnish the house. Bates concluded his letter by stating that the financial support of the entire society and of all Delawareans would be needed to preserve the Dutch House.[26]

## Chapter 6 – Historic Preservation in a Delaware Town

The society and the public responded enthusiastically. In January 1938, the underwriters' money was refunded because the purchase price had been raised from contributions. Restoration went on through 1938. Furnished with period artifacts, most provided by society member Louise du Pont Crowninshield, the restored house was included in *New Castle, Delaware: 1651–1939*, a book published by the society that featured photographs of New Castle landmarks. By 1940, $7,500 had been contributed to the preservation of the Dutch House. In spite of that auspicious start, the Dutch House restoration was the Delaware Society for the Preservation of Antiquities's only project within the town of New Castle. The outbreak of World War II put a damper on the society's activities, and the death of Mary Wilson Thompson shortly thereafter contributed to its demise. In 1948 or early 1949 the society turned its New Castle properties and other assets over to the New Castle Historical Society.[27]

Although the loss of the Delaware Society for the Preservation of Antiquities caused Bates some concern, it did not impede his efforts to preserve New Castle. Never one to rely on just a single plan of action, he pursued other means of reaching his goal even while he worked with the society. He remembered Electus Litchfield's emphasis on establishing a foundation to sponsor a survey of the town and identify sites worthy of preservation. And he remembered Litchfield's recommendation that Philip Laird be included on the committee to organize that foundation.[28]

Philip Laird had a keen interest in the formation of such a foundation. He wanted to assure the preservation of the Read House by giving the property to such an organization, subject to the Lairds' retention of life interest. Toward that end he began corresponding with Bates's friend Andrew Hepburn regarding a systematic preservation of New Castle. Hepburn in turn arranged for Kenneth Chorley, president of Colonial Williamsburg, to come to New Castle to meet with Laird and Bates. Chorley, enthusiastic about New Castle's possibilities, reiterated Litchfield's suggestion that a comprehensive survey must be the first order of business. To capture the imagination of a potential benefactor, skillfully rendered sketches of a fully restored town would say what words could not. The existence of Colonial Williamsburg proved this, for it was just such a portfolio that secured Rockefeller's backing for that project.[29]

Chorley's reference to Rockefeller echoed Goodwin's earlier caution, but others pondered the question of sponsorship as well. In 1938, an anonymous letter in the *Sunday Star* spoke of the need for a benefactor to renovate and preserve New Castle's wharf area, claiming that the town could vie with Williamsburg if a sponsor could be found to finance the work.[30] Yet some residents were not inclined to have New Castle systematically restored. Many families had roots in the town that reached back generations and were proud of the town just as it was. Perhaps some resented the interference of a newcomer like Laird, or the meddlesomeness of an outsider like Bates. Possibly they questioned the men's motivation. Laird owned several choice properties in New Castle. Then in 1939, through his newly organized New Castle Improvements Corporation, he purchased the Jefferson House on the Strand to renovate as a colonial inn and restaurant. He informed potential investors that Battery Park, recently acquired by the city, would be cleaned up in the near future, and that all buildings in the park and on the wharf adjoining the Jefferson House property should be removed as well, allowing hotel guests a fine view of the river. Laird's membership on the Battery Park Commission put him in an influential position, and as the proprietor of a colonial inn in the heart of a restored New Castle, he stood to profit handsomely.[31] Bates reported to Hepburn that "some of the New Castle people are not very enthusiastic about Mr. Laird's plans."[32]

One part of the plan about which Laird was not enthusiastic was the cost for the preliminary drawings. Andrew Hepburn told the New Castle group that a set of presentation sketches could be prepared for about $15,000. Chorley explained that this outlay would be an investment against future gate receipts, which while

## Chapter 6 – Historic Preservation in a Delaware Town

not on the scale of Williamsburg's, could be sizeable.[33] All agreed that the sketches were essential, but as they debated the feasibility of obtaining the necessary funds, World War II began, putting the project on hold.

After the war, the prospects for New Castle changed somewhat. Perry, Shaw, and Hepburn, now well known for their work at Williamsburg and other sites, increased their fee for the comprehensive survey to $20,000. At the same time, the project took on an air of greater urgency as spreading industrial development encroached upon New Castle.[34] Finally, Philip Laird's involvement in the project diminished due to illness. It fell to Daniel Moore Bates to carry the plan forward.

Bates realized that the chances of success were limited if they depended solely upon his resources. He turned for assistance to his friend Louise du Pont Crowninshield, already known in New Castle for her efforts to preserve the Dutch House on Third Street for the Delaware Society for the Preservation of Antiquities. He informed her in September 1946 that Perry, Shaw, and Hepburn were prepared to do a preliminary survey and additional research work if the $20,000 they required could be raised. "I am so much interested in the New Castle project," he continued, "that with your backing of experience and interest and such financial help as you may be able to give, I am prepared to underwrite."[35] She responded that she thought it a marvelous project and one she hoped would be successful, but that her own investment would be small because of her involvement with other charitable endeavors.[36] In spite of that cautious response, Bates immediately linked Mrs. Crowninshield's name to his own as cosponsor of the New Castle project.

Bates wasted no time in sending out a confidential letter informing some few "representative residents" of New Castle that an opportunity was forthcoming at which a small group of interested persons could meet with Andrew Hepburn and Kenneth Chorley to discuss options. Those invited to the meeting, held at the Amstel

House, had already demonstrated an interest in preservation through leadership in the New Castle Historical Society and the Delaware Society for the Preservation of Antiquities. The letter began Bates's selective involvement of influential people in his plans, a practice that he followed meticulously and that rewarded his efforts.[37] Bates reported to Mrs. Crowninshield that the meeting was a success. He wrote glowingly of the inspiring presentation given by Kenneth Chorley, who appealed to the company's sense of noblesse oblige in urging them to preserve their town for the benefit of generations to come.[38] To Andrew Hepburn, he wrote of his astonishment "at the enthusiastic reception of the idea by the people representing New Castle who were at the meeting."[39] Believing he now possessed the interest necessary to carry out his plan (and hoping that the financial backing would follow), Bates, with Chorley acting as advisor, made a contract with Perry, Shaw, and Hepburn to begin their survey.

Bates labored unceasingly for the next two and one half years to bring the survey to the point at which it could be presented to the public. The work progressed under the umbrella of Historic Research, Inc., a nonprofit corporation that Bates established so that contributions to the preservation effort would be deductible from the income taxes of the donors. Nevertheless, the greatest stumbling block proved to be obtaining financial backing. Anxious to make the report public in hopes that more money would thus be forthcoming, Bates chafed at having to keep the work secret to keep real estate speculators from moving in. A letter sent out to potential benefactors, including several du Ponts, proved unsuccessful. Responses such as H. F. du Pont's were typical: he wrote that while interested and happy to give some time to the project, his financial contribution would necessarily be small because his funds were committed elsewhere. Others, while interested, did not wish to be publicly associated with the project. Lammot du Pont Copeland contributed to the effort, but when Bates wanted to list him as an underwriter, he refused, stating that merely showing interest did not make him a

## Chapter 6 – Historic Preservation in a Delaware Town

sponsor. The greatest single contribution that Bates received was not monetary, but rather the generosity of Louise Crowninshield in allowing her name to be associated with the project. She realized that Bates needed a name attached to his endeavor that would draw others to the bandwagon, if only in the interest of vicarious association. Unfortunately, prestige alone did not pay the architects. In the end, Bates contributed over $15,000 to the cost of the survey. He wrote to a friend, "Sometimes this New Castle work ... has made me feel like a traveler along a lonely road."[40]

In addition to paying for the bulk of Perry, Shaw, and Hepburn's work through his firm Historic Research, Inc., Bates found himself contributing to other associated activities, hoping to see some return from his efforts. He arranged for some New Castle merchants and councilmen to go to Williamsburg to see the commercial prosperity that resulted from the restoration there. He also paid at least part of the cost for the "loan" of Perry, Shaw, and Hepburn to the New Castle Presbyterian Church, then undergoing a simultaneous, but ostensibly unrelated, restoration of its church building built in 1707.[41]

As the time neared for the report of Perry, Shaw, and Hepburn to be publicized, Bates focused his attention upon its format and presentation. He told Andrew Hepburn that he questioned the partners' decision to stress the architectural importance of the New Castle buildings, as he believed emphasis on their historical importance would have more appeal for the general public.[42] As a result, historian Jeannette Eckman joined the project.[43] Her research into the histories of New Castle properties dispelled some myths and provided the final report with another hook by which to capture the townsfolk's attention.

Bates also stressed that the actual presentation at a public meeting would need to be visually strong, suggesting the use of slides, diagrams, and photographs to attract attention. He desired some sort of publication, a brochure or pamphlet, that could be distributed at the meeting and which would summarize important points. Here Bates turned for advice to Charles Lee Reese, managing editor of the Wilmington *News-Journal* and member of the Delaware Society for the Preservation of Antiquities, and his colleague Anthony Higgins, who had written the text of *New Castle, Delaware: 1651–1939*. Reese suggested a question-and-answer format that would address why preservation should be undertaken, what had already been done, what remained to be done, and how an individual might contribute. He also suggested including in the pamphlet postcard reproductions of some of the restoration projects proposed for New Castle, including the restored shop fronts on Delaware Street and a resurrected Tile House on the Strand, to serve as visual reminders of the goals of the project.[44] In addition, he recommended that Bates contact Nicholas McIntire, editor of the *New Castle Gazette,* to enlist his assistance with further publicity and development. The decision to involve the local newsmen at the start of the project proved invaluable. In the months leading up to the presentation of the report, McIntire often touted the historic and architectural value of New Castle in his paper and encouraged the preservation of New Castle's buildings as a way to insure prosperity. Once the report was made public, both he and Reese wrote favorable editorials on the subject for their respective papers and provided complimentary reviews of the progress made.

The report of the preliminary survey by Perry, Shaw, and Hepburn was announced at a meeting held June 15, 1949, in the Old Academy on the Green in New Castle. The date appears an inspired choice, for on that same day in Washington, Congressman J. Hardin Peterson of Florida introduced into the House of Representatives Bill No. 5170 calling for "public participation in the preservation of sites, buildings, and objects of national significance or interest and providing a national trust for historic preservation."[45] In actuality, Bates had wanted to have the meeting back in May, around the time of "A Day in Old New Castle," but June 15 was the only day on

## Chapter 6 – Historic Preservation in a Delaware Town

which both Hepburn and Chorley could attend. Bates felt it imperative that these men be present, Hepburn because he had prepared so much of the report, and Chorley because he was Chorley. Williamsburg's president knew how to arouse an audience and he gave full measure to the several hundred citizens who attended the meeting. He described them as trustees who had the responsibility of preserving New Castle's old buildings for the future. He addressed their economic sensibilities by describing the prosperity that Williamsburg experienced after undergoing systematic restoration. Finally he appealed to their sense of patriotism:

> Upon completion of your plan, New Castle will become a reminder that one of the greatest faiths of all ages of civilized man is the faith we know today as Democracy.... The physical measure of our achievement as a people is merely an evidence of the tremendous constructive force which comes into existence when men and women are free to think, to speak, to achieve.... If you believe in your heritage; if you believe that the future may learn from the past; if you believe that the question of human liberty and freedom is 'unfinished business'; if you believe in Democracy; if you believe in the future of this country and of the world... then I look forward with every confidence to the day when New Castle will stand restored and preserved as one more beacon light and symbol of free men.[46]

Andrew Hepburn described the survey, explaining the rating of buildings in the proposed historic section and emphasizing that because of the wonderful care townsfolk had bestowed upon their property, very few structures were slated for removal.[47] "What you have," he told them, "is so great that all you have to do is preserve it." Hepburn described the plan not as a mandate, but as a resource for residents, even for those who might put off restoration for some time.[48] The whole event was well orchestrated. Bates was careful to plant people in the audience to ask questions, and he chose Judge Rodney, a familiar and respected figure in the town, to preside over the meeting.

In general, the response to the presentation was overwhelmingly positive. Bates received many glowing letters, and favorable reviews appeared in the local and Wilmington papers. In the following weeks, only one letter appeared in the *New Castle Gazette* questioning the wisdom of the proposal. The anonymous writer protested, "I can not understand how it is proposed to destroy a number of the buildings... listed for removal from the present scene.... [I]t just does not seem logical... to destroy buildings of a sturdy type that are serving a useful purpose. I think that many others who think through the proposal will see this as I do." Nicholas McIntire responded, "The ultimate aim is not to tear down buildings, but to replace... structures which are incongruous.... Our own personal feeling is, that some buildings which have been marked for eventual removal, might possibly be remodeled...."[49]

The protester had cause for concern, considering the scope of the project. Hepburn played down the magnitude of the proposed restoration, but the plan called for demolishing some fifty buildings. Fifty more were to be altered. Many structures slated for removal were important in the life of the community, including the library, the Masonic Hall, the Hotel Louise, the New Castle Club, the Presbyterian Church built in 1854, and an entire block of houses north of Harmony Street. Nicholas McIntire, who supported the plan, unintentionally revealed the importance of some of those buildings when he suggested renovation rather than demolition. Elsewhere he noted that some residents undoubtedly would feel nostalgic at the loss of the familiar landmarks.[50] In a related vein, James Eliason, president of the Board of Trustees of the New Castle Presbyterian Church, had written to Bates shortly after the congregation voted to restore the colonial church and demolish the 1854 building. He was eager to proceed with the work before members

## Chapter 6 – Historic Preservation in a Delaware Town

had time to reflect on how much the Gothic church had meant in their lives, and regret their decision to tear it down.[51]

Few people publicly protested the restoration scheme, in part because most buildings slated for demolition were less than one hundred years old. Many Americans at mid-century reacted to the turmoil of industrialization and global responsibility with nostalgia for the perceived simplicity of preindustrial life. Thus they revered artifacts of the colonial era and despised those from the more recent past. Many New Castilians participated fully in that colonial revivalist ideal. McIntire's and Eliason's words nevertheless reflected Bates's concern that the project be proposed in a way that would avoid alienating residents opposed to change. Thus Hepburn touted how much of the town would remain intact, rather than how much would be altered. Two years later, after various restoration projects were already underway in accordance with the plan, Mrs. J. Danforth Bush, in an address before the National Council for Historic Sites and Buildings, still emphasized, "We do not intend to rebuild the town in one fell swoop, we would be run out of town if we tried."[52]

Although Bates received many favorable comments following the presentation, a major benefactor did not appear. This was a crushing blow. He had counted on all of the good publicity to entice someone to take on the challenge of restoring New Castle, but all his corporation, reincorporated as Historic New Castle, Inc., received to carry out the program was a single endowment grant of $1000.[53] Nevertheless, Bates did not give up hope entirely. He still had a few cards left to play. First, he looked to Lydia Laird.

Long before the June meeting, Bates had been communicating with Lydia Laird about the possibility of her relinquishing her New Castle properties to his company for preservation, thus fulfilling the desire that her husband Philip had expressed back in 1940. He had died in 1947, but Bates credited him with inspiring his pursuit of the preservation of New Castle. He assured Lydia Laird that a way could be found by which she would retain life interest in the properties, yet at the same time create "a Foundation in memory of your husband and yourself which would insure old New Castle's going on through the years intact and beautiful and ever grateful to the Laird family for making possible its lasting conservation."[54] Bates enlisted the aid of Kenneth Chorley, who explained to Laird at length the process by which Williamsburg residents retained life tenancy in their historic homes while at the same time enjoying freedom from property taxes, insurance payments, and maintenance costs. Lydia Laird repeatedly expressed her interest in carrying out her husband's wishes, even publicly stating her desire to give the Read House to a foundation, but she could not bring herself to take action. Bates blamed the financial circumstances of Historic New Castle, Inc. Since he had been unable to obtain sufficient backing to guarantee the company's solvency, he did not blame Laird for her reluctance to entrust the care of her properties to the firm. Equally frustrating for him was the realization that if she could be enticed to give the Read House to Historic New Castle, Inc., her gift would be the galvanizing force the firm needed to attract more benefactors.[55]

Failing in his negotiations with Lydia Laird, Bates focused his attention upon the upcoming celebration of the tercentenary of the founding of New Castle, as he believed the excitement created by the celebration might be transferred to his preservation plans. Unfortunately, there did not appear to be much interest in the tercentenary among New Castle's residents. Once again, it fell to Bates to get the ball rolling. His associate, Jeannette Eckman, wrote a letter to the *Sunday Morning Star* "after waiting till the last hour for New Castle people to make the move," urging the celebration of the New Castle tercentenary and the appropriation of funds by the state legislature to establish a commission to plan the events. Her efforts resulted in a $5,000 appropriation, which Bates dismissed as "a paltry sum," stating that he had hoped for an appropriation of up to $100,000 to do major restoration on the old Court House.[56]

## Chapter 6 – Historic Preservation in a Delaware Town

Not one to be daunted by lack of funds, Bates took on the task of planning a tercentenary celebration for New Castle, even traveling to the Netherlands to arrange participation by the Dutch government. He also leapt at the opportunity to have an exhibit at the Library of Congress that would honor New Castle's tercentenary. Among the items included in the exhibit were Perry, Shaw, and Hepburn's illustrations of a restored New Castle.[57] Bates considered the celebration and the exhibit his best opportunity to generate national interest in New Castle, resulting, he hoped, in a benefactor coming forward.

When no "angel," as Bates described his non-existent benefactor, revealed himself after the tercentenary celebration, Bates turned his attention to the old Court House. The restoration of the Court House had been a priority to Bates since the contract discussions with Perry, Shaw, and Hepburn in 1946, although he found it expedient to support other projects, such as the restoration of the Presbyterian Church and the alterations to the shop facades on Delaware Street, rather than push for the Court House restoration due to the extreme cost of that undertaking. At the time of the tercentenary, more people began to call for the restoration of that his-

*Perry, Shaw, and Hepburn's sketch of the proposed restoration of Delaware Street opposite Market Street, 1947.*
*(Courtesy of the Historical Society of Delaware.)*

toric structure. The old building housed a restaurant, which, some feared, might be a fire hazard; it was Bates's intention that once the building was restored and preserved, it would be taken over by Historic New Castle, Inc., to operate as a museum. Although the Court House was owned by the state, provision had been made for its operation as a museum in 1915. Even at that early date, the building was recognized as being of significant historic value and worthy of preservation. The state legislature passed a resolution providing that "... if any Historical Society now incorporated or that may be incorporated under the laws of the State desires to use the said old State House at New Castle for administrative and museum purposes, that the commissioners... shall turn the building over to the said Historical Society."[58]

Although there was widespread interest in restoring the Court House, the cost factor and the governmental red tape were daunting. The preliminary survey alone, necessary before restoration could begin, cost $18,000. A benefactor for this project did appear in the person of H. Rodney Sharp, well known among Delaware preservationists for his restoration of the town of Odessa. Louise Crowninshield managed to interest Sharp in the project, and he offered to put up half of the funds required by Perry, Shaw, and Hepburn to do the job. Having failed in his efforts to get Lydia Laird to donate the Read House to Historic New Castle, Inc., Bates saw the Court House project as his final chance to demonstrate the validity of his intentions. He wrote to Sharp that his offer was just the spark needed to get New Castle "on its mettle," and that he hoped assistance would be forthcoming from the Trustees of New Castle Common through Bates's influence with trustees sympathetic to his endeavour. Not willing to rely even on his close associates to provide the rest of the money, Bates told Sharp in confidence that while he was not feeling too financially secure at the moment, he valued the opportunity to save the Court House and would provide the other $9,000 himself.[59] Louise Crowninshield then offered to con-

## Chapter 6 – Historic Preservation in a Delaware Town

tribute half of Bates's share, but ultimately the Trustees of New Castle Common did come through, and neither Bates nor Crowninshield had to contribute towards the project. Even so, the preliminary survey revealed that a difficult and expensive project was at hand. The restoration took years, and once again Bates lost the opportunity to have a significant restoration project associated with Historic New Castle, Inc.

Although Bates failed to secure a sound financial base for his firm, he did triumph in obtaining zoning regulations for the town. This had been a primary goal of his since the 1930s and by 1950 the townspeople agreed that the town center should be protected from undesirable development. Their motivation was not necessarily preservation of the historic buildings for their own sake. One faction wanted to force a long-established tavern out of business because it operated in what they considered to be a residential district.[60] Many businessmen desired a restored town because they had been informed repeatedly by Bates and others of Williamsburg's prosperity. Yet increasingly people came to favor preservation because they saw New Castle as a place worth protecting.

In the early 1950s the New Castle City Council turned to Bates for advice on establishing suitable zoning ordinances. He secured for them copies of zoning ordinances from Williamsburg and other historic cities which served as the models for New Castle's plan. New Castle's proposal included establishing a board of architectural review to include at least two city residents and an architect recognized as a specialist on historic buildings. Town meetings enabled residents to voice their opinions regarding the proposed ordinances, with favorable results. The only criticism in the local paper came from realtors, who disliked the strict setback requirements for new construction. Most residents within the proposed historic district approved the proposal, and some asked that the boundaries of the historic section, where the strictest regulations would pertain, be enlarged. This delighted Bates as it displayed the growing support for preservation.[61]

In spite of his success with the zoning ordinances, Bates's inability to obtain either a benefactor for New Castle or a major restoration project for Historic New Castle, Inc., was a constant frustration for him. By the early 1950s he was seriously considering curtailing his activity in New Castle and in historic preservation in general. After a serious automobile accident left him hospitalized for months early in 1952, Bates wrote Louise Crowninshield that he had in recent years been "endeavoring to get out of my various commitments and responsibilities in this and other connections."[62] Crowninshield was unwilling to let him go so easily and tempted him with a request to accept membership on the National Council of Historic Sites and Buildings' regional committee for the mid-Atlantic states. As a member of the National Council since 1949, Bates felt such respect for the organization and the efforts Louise Crowninshield had made on its behalf that he accepted the position.[63] However, by 1953 he desired to withdraw as president of Historic New Castle, Inc., and turn the mantle of authority over to another of the firm's trustees, Daniel Wolcott; but Wolcott protested, saying "You are the driving force which has progressed the matter thus far."[64] It was not for Bates to carry the matter any further, however, as he died in Wilmington on February 23, 1953.

By 1953, Daniel Moore Bates likely considered his efforts to preserve New Castle only partially successful. In a letter to Andrew Hepburn in 1948, Bates outlined his priorities for New Castle. They included the restoration of the early-eighteenth-century Presbyterian Church and the removal of its mid-nineteenth-century counterpart, the restoration of the shops along Delaware Street, the removal of the old library and the Masonic Hall, the reconstruction of the Tile House, the restoration of the Court House, and the building of a colonial-style hotel on Battery Park adjacent to the town.[65] Five years later, the Presbyterian Church had been restored and work was underway on the Court House, but these accomplishments had been achieved without a substantial contribution from Historic New

## Chapter 6 – Historic Preservation in a Delaware Town

Castle, Inc., as the firm had never obtained an endowment sufficient to fund any restoration project. Likewise several buildings on Delaware Street and elsewhere in town had been restored, but by their owners rather than by Bates's corporation.

While Bates chafed at his role as advisor and strove to obtain the financial backing that would enable him to take a more active part in the preservation of New Castle, it is probable that he failed to see the significance of his contribution to the town. While there were earlier scattered attempts at preservation in New Castle through the work of Laussat Rogers, Philip Laird, the New Castle Historical Society, and the Delaware Society for the Preservation of Antiquities, Bates's years of concentrated activity galvanized efforts to preserve the town. His decision to involve national players in the field of preservation such as Kenneth Chorley and the architectural firm of Perry, Shaw, and Hepburn made New Castle's people more fully aware of their town's historic significance and encouraged their efforts to preserve it.

Modern preservationists are relieved that the "restoration" plan espoused by Bates and Perry, Shaw, and Hepburn, which advocated

*Perry, Shaw, and Hepburn's sketch of the proposed restoration of the Strand, including the rebuilt Tile House, 1947.*
*(Courtesy of the Historical Society of Delaware.)*

demolishing many significant buildings, never came to fruition, for it would have resulted in a fantasy town that presented a false history of New Castle. Such selective history was typical of the colonial revivalist ideals of the first half of the twentieth century, but now preservationists recognize that all buildings have their stories to tell, that no single time period is more "historical" than another, and that a community's vitality over the centuries is discernible only when all of its architectural and cultural manifestations are respected.

Today most of New Castle's architectural gems from all time periods remain more or less intact, but support for preservation is not universal. Some residents still consider Victorian buildings unworthy of special consideration. They chafe at the restrictions that come with living in the historic district and would have them lifted on houses dating from the post-colonial era. Several Victorian-era buildings have been demolished, some quite recently, and replaced with bland pseudo-colonial structures or with mini-parks that leave telling gaps in the streetscapes. Other buildings are threatened. Yet many residents take pride in the city's diverse architectural heritage. Nicholas McIntire often wrote in the *New Castle Gazette* about the annual "Day in Old New Castle" celebration, fondly calling it "Colonial Day," but that term is inappropriate today, when restored Victorian homes are also proudly displayed to the visiting public.

It was largely for the "visiting public" that Daniel Moore Bates and his associates sought to preserve New Castle. Their motives were admirable by the preservation standards of their day, for they truly believed that they were performing a service to the American people, one that would foster a sense of patriotism while providing a stabilizing influence in a rapidly changing world. Yet the real credit for the town one sees today lies with the residents, who, while inspired by the early preservationists, ultimately demonstrated a broader vision. They see New Castle not as a relic from the past, but as a vibrant community whose story continues to unfold and choose to protect it not as a museum, but because it is their home.

## Chapter 6 – Historic Preservation in a Delaware Town

[1] "Mayor Klingmeyer Urges City Update Its Comprehensive Plan," *New Castle Eagle,* Apr. 4, 1990.

[2] Worthington G. Button to Daniel Moore Bates (hereafter DMB), Jan 16, 1951, Bates Family Papers, Box 69, Historical Society of Delaware, Wilmington (hereafter referred to as Bates 69), All Bates papers are at the Historical Society of Delaware (hereafter HSD) unless otherwise noted.

[3] Charles B. Hosmer, Jr, *Presence of the Past: A History of the Preservation Movement in the United States Before Williamsburg* (New York, 1965), p. 22.

[4] William B. Rhoads, "The Colonial Revival and the Americanization of Immigrants," in *The Colonial Revival in America,* ed. Alan Axelrod (New York, 1985), p. 341.

[5] Charles B. Hosmer, *Preservation Comes of Age: From Williamsburg to the National Trust, 1926–1949,* 2 vols. (Charlottesville, 1981), 1:2.

[6] Ibid.

[7] John Watson, *Annals of Philadelphia and Pennsylvania,* 1844 edition, 2 vols., 2:539, cited in Thomas Beckman to Roderick Blackburn, Jan. 3, 1986, museum registrar's file, "Tile House—New Castle 1687 date irons," HSD.

[8] Beckman to Blackburn, Jan. 3, 1986, museum registrar's file, "Tile House—New Castle 1687 date irons," HSD.

[9] Laussat Richter Rogers (1866–1957) was born in California but had close family ties to New Castle. After completing training as an architect in the 1890s, he returned to New Castle to live at Boothurst, his family home just outside of town. An advocate of the colonial revival style of architecture, he was involved in several preservation projects in the town in the early twentieth century. He also founded the *New Amstel Magazine* in 1908, by which he claimed credit for "rescuing from oblivion the name of New Amstel" (Gene E. Harris, biographical essay in *Laussat Richter Rogers* [Chadds Ford, Pa., 1986], pp. 7–15).

[10] Conversation with Kathy Bratton, director, New Castle Historical Society, May 21, 1990.

[11] Christopher M. Agnew, "A Brief Architectural History of Immanuel Church" in *God With Us: a Continuing Presence and the Vital Records Taken from the Parish Registers of Immanuel Church, New Castle, Delaware,* ed. Christopher M. Agnew (New Castle, Del., 1986), p. 2.

[12] *Wilmington Every Evening,* Nov. 23, 1918, cited in Agnew, p. 2.

[13] Timothy J. Mullin, "In the Spirit of the Original: Fantasizing about the 18th Century with Phillip [sic] and Lydia Laird," interpretive essay, Mar. 1987 (hereafter cited as Mullin), p. 9, George Read II House, HSD.

[14] *Wilmington Every Evening,* Jun. 23, 1920, cited in Mullin.

[15] Lydia Laird gave the Read House to the Historical Society of Delaware in 1975. Since then it has undergone a thorough restoration to its early-nineteenth-century appearance, even to the restoration of the original brilliant paint colors, but the dining room, basement taproom, and one bedroom have been left as decorated by Lydia Laird in recognition of her generosity.

[16] Anthony Higgins, *New Castle, Delaware, 1651–1939* (Boston, 1939), p. 4.

[17] Open letter from Mary E. Shaw, Harriett M. Cavenaugh, Annie R. Janvier, C. Douglass Buck, Philip Laird, Richard S. Rodney, Mar. 5, 1929, files of the New Castle Historical Society (hereafter referred to as NCHS).

[18] From a New Castle family of long standing, Judge Richard S. Rodney (1882–1963) lived on Third Street and was intensely interested in anything relating to New Castle history. Elected president of the New Castle Historical Society in 1934, he held the position until his death in 1963. Francis Janvier (1874–1940) came from another old New Castle family. C. Douglass Buck (1890–1965) served as governor of Delaware from 1929 to 1937.

[19] Letter from C. Douglass Buck, Philip Laird, Francis deH. Janvier, and Richard S. Rodney addressed "To the Patrons of Amstel House," Dec. 4, 1931, NCHS files; minutes of the board of directors, Dec. 19, 1931, minute book, NCHS; and certificate of incorporation, Jun. 1934, NCHS files.

[20] DMB to Mary Wilson Thompson, Dec. 31, 1936, Bates 69, Delaware Society for the Preservation of Antiquities (hereafter referred to as DSPA) file.

[21] DMB to Andrew H. Hepburn, Apr. 10, 1946, Bates 69, Hepburn & Perry, Shaw, and Hepburn from Nov. 1, 1946 file.

[22] DMB to Electus D. Litchfield, Jun. 1933, Bates 69, DSPA file.

[23] W. A. R. Goodwin to DMB, Mar. 23, 1934, Bates 69, DSPA file.

[24] DMB to Andrew H. Hepburn, May 5, 1937, Bates 69, DSPA file.

[25] Electus D. Litchfield to Mary Wilson Thompson, Jun. 1937, Bates 69, DSPA file.

[26] DMB to Alfred E. Bissell, Dec. 12, 1937, Bates 69, Laird file; and DMB to W. A. R. Goodwin, Jul. 13, 1937, and DMB to Mrs. H. B. Thompson, Philip Laird, Alfred E. Bissell, Mrs. Francis deH. Janvier, and H. Rodney Sharp, Dec. 27, 1937, Bates 69, DSPA file.

[27] DMB to Alfred E. Bissell, Jan. 1, 1938, Bates 69, DSPA file; "Dutch House Will Be Open to Public Tomorrow," *New Castle Gazette,* Jun. 15, 1951; Alfred

## Chapter 6 – Historic Preservation in a Delaware Town

E. Bissell to DMB Jun. 1940, Bates 69, DSPA file; memorandum of ca. 1946, Bates Family Papers, Box 68 (hereafter referred to as Bates 68); and minutes of board of directors, Jan. 20, 1949, minute book, NCHS. The Delaware Society for the Preservation of Antiquities was reestablished in the 1960s. It now operates the Hale-Byrnes House, an historic house located in Stanton.

[28] Electus D. Litchfield to Mary Wilson Thompson, Jun. 1937, Bates 69, DSPA file.

[29] DMB to Kenneth Chorley, Nov. 15, 1948, Bates 69, Laird file; and Hosmer, *Preservation Comes of Age,* 1:69.

[30] *Wilmington Sunday Star,* May 29, 1938, clipping in Bates 68.

[31] Philip D. Laird to DMB, Oct. 26, 1939, Bates 69, Laird file. Laird stated that considering the historic interest in New Castle, it was necessary that there be an attractive inn for people to visit, and for this purpose he formed the New Castle Improvements Corporation. The new firm was a completely separate entity with no ties to Laird and Co.

[32] DMB to Andrew H. Hepburn, Oct. 1, 1940, cited in Mullin, p. 12.

[33] Hosmer, *Preservation Comes of Age,* 1:69.

[34] Andrew H. Hepburn, "New Castle," introductory essay to the Preliminary Survey by Perry, Shaw, and Hepburn, Architects, Dec. 22, 1947, HSD.

[35] DMB to Louise du Pont Crowninshield, Sep. 3, 1946, Bates 68, New Castle—Crowninshield correspondence file.

[36] Louise du Pont Crowninshield to DMB, Sep. 13, 1946, Bates 68, New Castle—Crowninshield correspondence file.

[37] DMB and Louise du Pont Crowninshield to potential sponsors, Oct. 3, 1946, Bates 68, New Castle Historical Society file. The potential sponsors included Mr. and Mrs. Newlin Booth, Mr. and Mrs. J. Danforth Bush, Jr., Mr. John J. B. Cooper, Miss Mary Cooper, Mr. and Mrs. Horace Deakyne, Mr. and Mrs. James T. Eliason, Jr., Mr. and Mrs. J. Rogers Holcomb, Mr. and Mrs. Thomas Holcomb 3rd, Mr. Albert Kruse, Miss Gertrude Kruse, Mr. and Mrs. Philip D. Laird, and Mr. and Mrs. Richard S. Rodney.

[38] DMB to Louise du Pont Crowninshield, Oct. 29, 1946, Bates 68, New Castle Historical Society file.

[39] DMB to Andrew H. Hepburn, Oct. 28, 1946, Bates 68, Correspondence—Hepburn file.

[40] DMB to Andrew H. Hepburn, Jun. 26, 1946, Bates 68, New Castle … the New Castle Historical Society meeting file; Henry Francis du Pont to DMB, Nov. 27, 1946, Winterthur Archives, Box 248, "Daniel Moore Bates," Winterthur Museum, Winterthur, Delaware; Lammot du Pont Copeland to DMB, Jan. 19, 1949, Bates 68, New Castle—Misc. Correspondence 1949 file; Louise du Pont Crowninshield to DMB, Jan. 18, 1949, Bates 69,

Crowninshield correspondence 1949 file; DMB to Andrew H. Hepburn, Nov. 3, 1948, Bates 68, Hepburn and Perry, Shaw, and Hepburn correspondence, Report file; and DMB to Katherine Callery, Jun. 18, 1949, Bates 68.

[41] DMB to Henry N. Haut, Oct. 22, 1948, Bates 68, New Castle—Shops file. In fact the two projects were closely allied through the association of Bates and James T. Eliason, Jr., president of the Board of Trustees of the New Castle Presbyterian Church (Bates 68, New Castle Presbyterian Church file).

[42] DMB to Andrew H. Hepburn, Apr. 21, 1937, Bates 68, New Castle Report file.

[43] Jeannette Eckman (1882–1972) was known for her untiring research in New Castle where she supervised the Delaware Federal Writers' Project that resulted in the publication of *Delaware: a Guide to the First State* (1938) and *New Castle on the Delaware* (1936).

[44] DMB to Andrew H. Hepburn, Sep. 10, 1947, and DMB to Hepburn, Oct. 22, 1948, Bates 68, New Castle Report file.

[45] U S., Congress, House, *A Bill to Further the Policy Enunciated in the Historic Sites Act (49 Stat. 666) and to Facilitate Public Participation in the Preservation of Sites, Buildings, and Objects of National Significance or Interest and Providing a National Trust for Historic Preservation*, H.R. 5170, 81st Cong., 1st sess., 1949, p. 1.

[46] "Restoration Project Is Seen As Leading to Great Prosperity," *New Castle Gazette*, Jun. 17, 1949.

[47] The Preliminary Report compiled by Perry, Shaw, and Hepburn consisted of scale drawings of the front elevations of all houses within the designated historic area "A" along with considerable historical background on each house compiled by Jeannette Eckman. It also included a plan of Historic area "A" indicating which houses were to be preserved ("P"), altered ("A"), and removed ("R"), and some sketches of proposed restorations, along with procedural recommendations. Copies of the report may be seen at the Historical Society of Delaware, the New Castle Historical Society, and at the New Castle Public Library (photocopy).

[48] "Restoration Project Is Seen As Leading To Great Prosperity," *New Castle Gazette*, Jun. 17, 1949.

[49] Anonymous, "A Letter To The Editor," *New Castle Gazette*, Jun. 24, 1949.

[50] "New Castle is Talking About," *New Castle Gazette*, Jun. 17, 1949.

[51] James T. Eliason to DMB, May 20, 1947, and DMB to Andrew H. Hepburn, May 29, 1947, Bates 68, N. Castle—Old Presbyterian Church file.

[52] "New Castle Goes Forward with Restoration—A Review of Past Achievements and Present Plans," excerpts from a presentation by Mrs. J.

## Chapter 6 – Historic Preservation in a Delaware Town

Danforth Bush to the National Council for Historic Sites and Buildings, Oct. 19, 1951, in *New Castle Gazette,* Nov. 1951.

53 After the report of Perry, Shaw, and Hepburn was presented to the public, Historic Research, Inc., was reincorporated as Historic New Castle, Inc. Bates had felt it prudent to adopt the name Historic Research, Inc., so as to prevent tipping off real estate speculators to the interest in New Castle.

54 DMB to Lydia C. Laird, Mar. 1948, Bates 69, Laird file.

55 Kenneth Chorley to Lydia C. Laird, Jun. 20, 1949, memorandum of Jul. 14, 1949, and DMB to Kenneth Chorley, Jun. 9, 1950, Bates 69, Laird file.

56 Jeannette Eckman to DMB, Jun. 17, 1949, clipping from *Wilmington Sunday Morning Star,* Apr. 3, 1949, and DMB to Jeannette Eckman, Jun. 18, 1949, Bates 68, New Castle—Misc. Correspondence 1949.

57 *Old New Castle and Modern Delaware: The Tercentenary of the Founding of New Castle by the Dutch* (Washington, D.C., 1951).

58 "Old Capital, State's No. 1 Shrine, Target for Restoration," *New Castle Gazette,* Jun. 15, 1951. The 1915 legislation cited the building's status as the oldest courthouse in the country and concern that it be fireproofed as reasons for its preservation.

59 DMB to H. Rodney Sharp, Jul. 18, 1950, Bates 69, New Castle—H. Rodney Sharp file.

60 Clipping, "The Zoning Matter Illustrated," *New Castle Gazette,* Nov. 17, 1950, Bates 69, New Castle Clippings—Misc. file.

61 Undated memorandum, Bates 69, New Castle Misc. Correspondence 1951 file; clippings, "Public Hearing on Zoning Ordinance Scheduled Tuesday," *New Castle Gazette,* Oct. 19, 1951, and "New Castle Sets Zoning Meeting," *Wilmington Morning News,* Nov. 5, 1951, Bates 68, New Castle—Zoning file; and DMB to Henry N. Haut, Nov. 24, 1951, Bates 69, New Castle Misc. Correspondence 1951 file.

62 DMB to Louise du Pont Crowninshield, Apr. 11, 1952, Bates 69.

63 Louise du Pont Crowninshield to DMB, Jan. 23, 1952, and DMB to Louise du Pont Crowninshield, Apr. 11, 1952, Bates 69.

64 Daniel Wolcott to DMB, Jan. 7, 1953, Bates 69, Historic New Castle, Inc., 1949 file.

65 DMB to Andrew H. Hepburn, Dec. 15, 1948, Bates 68, Hepburn and Perry, Shaw, and Hepburn correspondence, Report file.

# Selected New Castle Bibliography Through 2001

*Stephen J. Cordano*

The following bibliography is by no means a comprehensive listing of every mention of New Castle contained in print. It is rather a selection of works in which there is a notable reference to the town, or which provide some special insight into the history, architecture, geography, and culture that define this national treasure.

Credit must be given to the efforts of Elizabeth Moyne, Harold Hancock, and Constance Cooper for their Delaware bibliographies that have appeared in *Delaware History* through the years, and the efforts of Paul William Kelly, whose New Castle bibliography of 1951 this compilation updates.

Able, Augustus Henry III. "Fiction as a Mirror of Delaware Life," *Delaware History* 3 (March 1948): 37–53.

Acrelius, Israel. "A History of New Sweden; or, The Settlements on the River Delaware," *Historical Society of Pennsylvania, Memoirs* 11 (1874): 468 pp.

Adeler, Max. *Out of the Hurly-Burly; or Life in an Odd Corner.* [pseud. of Charles Heber Clark.] Philadelphia, 1874. 398 pp.

Agnew, Christopher M., ed. *God With Us: A Continuing Presence and the Vital Records Taken from the Parish Registers of Immanuel Church, New Castle, Delaware.* New Castle, 1987. 158 pp.

"Amstel, Van Dyke and Chancellor Kensey Johns Houses," *Architectural Forum* 65 (August 1936): 125–132.

Arnold, Heather. *The Tides Led the Town: A Recent History of the Waterfront—New Castle Delaware*. New Castle [New Castle Historical Society], 1994. 29 pp.

Bankert, Jean E. *A History of New Castle Presbyterian Church 1651–1989*. n.p., 1989. 51 pp.

Belknap, Maitland. "The Town that Time Forgot," *Country Life*, October 1920, 42–45.

Bennett, George Fletcher. *Early Architecture of Delaware*. Introduction and text by Joseph L. Copeland. Wilmington, 1932. 213 pp.

———. *The Perennial Apprentice: Sixty Year Scrapbook, 1916 to 1976*. Wilmington, 1977. 233 pp.

Bird, Mary Mayer. *Life of Robert Montgomery Bird*. [of New Castle.] Philadelphia, 1945. 130 pp.

Bleiberg, Carl. "Dutch Education in New Amstel." *Federal Writers' Papers at the University of Delaware*, v. 11, pp. 1–4.

Boeschenstein, Warren. *Historic American Towns Along the Atlantic Coast*. Baltimore, 1999. 331 pp.

Booth, Elizabeth. *Reminiscences [of New Castle]*. New Castle, 1884. 202 pp.

Borah, Leo Arthur. "Diamond Delaware, Colonial Still," *National Geographic Magazine*, September 1935, 367–398.

Brandt, Francis Burke. *The Majestic Delaware: The Nation's Foremost Historic River*. Philadelphia, 1929. 192 pp.

"A Brief Sketch of the Military Operations on the Delaware During the War of 1812," *Delaware History* 3 (September 1948): 79–96.

*Bibliography*

Brown, Robert Frank. "Front Street, New Castle, Delaware: Architecture and Building Practices 1687–1859." Master's thesis, University of Delaware, 1961.

Browning, G. K. "Deed Mentioning Old New Castle Fort." *Federal Writers' Papers at the University of Delaware*, v. 4, pp. 358–359.

Buffington, Nancy. "African Americans in New Castle Through 1850," *Fully, Freely, & Entirely* [Delaware Heritage Commission] 11 (Winter 2000): 4–5.

Butler, Gordon. "New Castle." *Federal Writers' Papers at the University of Delaware*, v. 26, pp. 14–15.

Cable, George W. *A Short History of the First Baptist Church, New Castle, Delaware, 1876–1956.* n.p., n.d. 4 pp.

Caldwell, Robert Graham. *Red Hannah: Delaware's Whipping Post.* Philadelphia, 1947. 144 pp.

Cario, William Richard. "Anglicization in a 'Frenchified, Scotchified, Dutchified Place': New Castle, Delaware, 1690–1750." Ph.D. dissertation, New York University, 1994. 369 pp.

Carson, Hampton Lawrence. "Dutch and Swedish Settlements on the Delaware," *Pennsylvania Magazine of History and Biography* 33 (1909): 1–21.

Chappell, Jennifer. "Colonial Calm," *Coastal Living*, September–October 1999, 80–88.

"Charter of New Castle," *Delaware History* 3 (March 1948): 26–36.

Cheyney, James Barton. "New Castle Common-Penn's Gift." *Federal Writers' Papers at the University of Delaware*, v. 4, pp. 369–373.

Coatsworth, Elizabeth Jane. *The Big Green Umbrella.* New York, 1944. 26 pp.

Cohen, William J., et al. *Dobbinsville and the Surrounding Area: A Planning Study for the Future.* New Castle [Trustees of the New Castle Common], 1985. 58 pp.

Conner, William H. "British Peace Commission of 1778 Stayed at New Castle." *Federal Writers' Papers at the University of Delaware,* v. 1, pp. 271–273.

———. "New Castle in Literature." *Federal Writers' Papers at the University of Delaware,* v. 6, pp. 30–31.

———. "Sir Robert Carr and the Naming of New Castle." *Federal Writers' Papers at the University of Delaware,* v. 1, pp. 392–393.

Cooch, Edward Webb. *Delaware Historic Events, a Compilation of Articles and Addresses.* Cooch's Bridge, Del., 1946. 159 pp.

Cooper, Alexander B. "Fort Casimir: The Starting Point in the History of New Castle," Historical Society of Delaware Papers, no. 43. Wilmington, 1905. 39 pp.

———. "History of New Castle." *Wilmington Sunday Star,* serial that appeared from January 21, 1906–May 12, 1907.

———. *Methodism in New Castle, with a Few Incidents in the Ministerial Life of Rev. Ezekiel Cooper.* Wilmington, 1914. 32 pp.

Cooper, Constance J. "A Town Among Cities: New Castle, Delaware, 1780–1840." Ph.D. dissertation, University of Delaware, 1983. 342 pp.

Cottrell, Robert Curtice. "Town Planning in New Castle, Delaware, 1797–1838." Master's thesis, University of Delaware, 1991. 70 pp.

Crowe, Donald. "Early Industries in New Castle." *Federal Writers' Papers at the University of Delaware,* v. 24, pp. 169–172.

Crownfield, Gertrude. *King's Pardon.* Philadelphia, 1937. 317 pp.

*Bibliography*

_____. *Proud Lady.* Philadelphia, 1942. 259 pp.

*A Day in Old New Castle.* New Castle [Friends of Immanuel Church], various years. [guide to activities, open houses and gardens.]

Delaware Historic Markers Commission. *Guide to Historic Markers in Delaware.* Wilmington?, 1933. pp. 15–18.

Delaware Society for the Preservation of Antiquities. *History of the Oldest Dwelling in Delaware.* n.p., n.d. 4 pp. [Old Dutch House in New Castle.]

DiSabatino, Patricia Austin. *St. Peter's of New Castle 1804–1984.* n.p., n.d. 31 pp.

Dunlap, A. R. "Three Lists of Passengers to New Amstel," *Delaware History* 8 (1959): 310–311.

Eberlein, Harold Donaldson, and Courtlandt V. D. Hubbard. *Historic Houses and Buildings of Delaware.* Dover [Public Archives Commission], 1962. 227 pp.

Eckman, Jeannette. "Life Among the Early Dutch at New Castle," *Delaware History* 4 (June 1951): 246–302.

"Extracts from the Journal of a Traveller Passing Through the Village of New Castle, Oct. 1820," *Delaware Gazette,* October 17, 1820. p. 3; October 24, 1820. p. 2; November 3, 1820. p. 2.

Falter, John, illus. "Delaware Street, New Castle, Delaware," *The Saturday Evening Post*, March 17, 1962, cover illustration.

Faris, John Thomson. *Historic Shrines of America.* New York, 1918. pp. 203–208.

_____. "New Castle—The Town of Four Flags," *Delaware Motorist*, February 1933, 2–4.

Federal Writers' Project, Delaware. *Delaware, A Guide to the First State.* New York, 1938. [New Castle, pp. 232–252.]

———. *New Castle on the Delaware.* ed. by Jeannette Eckman. New Castle Historical Society, 1936. 142 pp.; Dutch Tercentenary Edition, 1651–1951, ed. by Jeannette Eckman. New Castle Historical Society, 1950. 151 pp.; ed. by Anthony Higgins. New Castle Historical Society, 1973. 175 pp.

Ferris, Benjamin. *A History of the Original Settlements on the Delaware.* Wilmington, 1846. 312 pp.

Fiske, Dorsey. *Raptor.* New York, 2000. 220 pp.

Foster, William D. *An Architectural Monograph: New Castle, Delaware, an Eighteenth Century Town.* New York, 1926. 13 pp. [White Pine Series, no. 65.]

Fryer, Aaron G. "The Story of New Castle," *Antiques* 60 (August 1951): 113–117.

Gallant, Kathleen Baker. *The Butcher, The Baker, The Aeroplane Maker: Business in New Castle, Delaware 1875–1950.* New Castle [New Castle Historical Society], 1995. 23 pp.

Gibson, George H., ed. *The Collected Essays of Richard S. Rodney on Early Delaware.* Wilmington, 1975. 278 pp.

Hamilton, Alexander. *Hamilton's Itinerarium; Being a Narrative of a Journey from Annapolis, Maryland, through Delaware ... from May to September, 1744.* St. Louis, 1907. 263 pp.

Hammond, John Martin. *Colonial Mansions of Maryland and Delaware.* Philadelphia, 1914. 304 pp.

Hammond, Reese. "Negroes in New Castle." *Federal Writers' Papers at the University of Delaware,* v. 29, pp. 205–207.

Harper, Deborah Van Riper. "'The Gospel of New Castle': Historic Preservation in a Delaware Town," *Delaware History* 25 (Fall–Winter 1992–93): 77–105.

# Bibliography

Harris, Bill. *Grand Homes of the Mid Atlantic States.* New York, 1989. 160 pp.

Hay, Henry Hanby. *Annals of Amstel House.* New Castle?, n.d. 12 pp.

Hayes, Jacob Carroll. "The Delaware Curve; The Story of the Pennsylvania-Delaware Circular Boundary," *Pennsylvania Magazine of History and Biography* 47 (1923): 238–258.

Heite, Edward F., and Louise B. Heite. *Report of Phase I Archeological Investigations at the Site of Fort Casimir.* Dover, Del. [Delaware Department of Transportation], 1986. 59 pp.

Heite, Louise B. "Garrison to County Seat: New Castle on the Delaware," *The Delaware Antiques Show*, 1978, 49–60.

———. "New Castle Under the Duke of York: A Stable Community." Master's thesis, University of Delaware, 1978. 179 pp.

Higgins, Anthony. "New Castle on the Delaware," *American Heritage*, Summer 1951, 18+.

*History of St. John's Lodge No. 2, A. F. & A. M., New Castle, Delaware, 1781–1935.* n.p., n.d. 40 pp. [Includes addresses by Richard S. Rodney and John Dickinson Read.]

Holcomb, Thomas. *Sketch of Early Ecclesiastical Affairs in New Castle, Delaware and History of Immanuel Church.* Wilmington, 1890. 254 pp.

Holmes, William F. "The New Castle and Frenchtown Turnpike and Railroad Company, 1809–1838," *Delaware History* 10 (1962–63): 71–104, 152–180, 235–270.

Howard, Hugh. *The Preservationist's Progress: Architectural Adventures in Conserving Yesterday's Houses.* New York, 1991. 272 pp.

Howard, Paige. "A Day in Old New Castle," *The Hunt*, April–May 1999, 71–75+.

Hubbard, Edward Lecompt. "History of the New Castle Methodist Episcopal Church." In *Asbury Methodist Episcopal Church, Wilmington. Centennial Services. Oct. 13–20, 1889*. Wilmington, 1889, pp. 287–291.

Janvier, Anne Read, comp. *Stories of Old New Castle.* New Castle, 1930. 43 pp.

Johnson, Amandus. *The Swedes on the Delaware, 1638–1664.* Philadelphia, 1914. 391 pp.

Keith, Lieut. Gov. Sir William. "First Report...to the Lords Commissioners for Trade and Plantations, 1717," *Pennsylvania Magazine of History and Biography* 23 (1899): 488–497. [Transactions with the Assembly at New Castle, pp. 491–497.]

Kelly, Paul William. New Castle, Delaware: *A Bibliography in Commemoration of the Tercentenary of the Founding of New Castle.* Newark, Del., 1951. 20 pp.

Kruse, Albert. "An Impression of the Old Manner of Building in New Castle, Delaware," *Delaware History* 4 (June 1951): 171–206.

_____. "Four Lithographs of New Castle," *Architecture* 70 (September 1934): 153–156.

_____. *New Castle Sketches.* Drawings by Albert Kruse, notes by Gertrude Kruse. Philadelphia, 1932. 31 pp.

Kuralt, Charles. *Dateline America.* New York, 1979. 224 pp.

Laird, Marnie. "The George Read II House," *Early American Life* 18:4 (1987), 62-68.

Larrimore, Lida. *Mulberry Square.* New York, 1930. 290 pp.

Lathrop, Elise L. *Early American Inns and Taverns.* New York, 1926. pp. 204–205.

_____. *Historic Houses of Early America.* New York, 1927. pp. 405–408.

# Bibliography

Lewis, Jack. *The Delaware Scene.* Wilmington, 1940. Unpaginated.

Lewis, John Frederick. *Thomas Spry, Lawyer and Physician.* Philadelphia, 1932. 126 pp.

Library of Congress. *Old New Castle and Modern Delaware.* Washington, D.C., 1951. 59 pp.

Lore, Charles Brown. "Life and Character of Edward W. Gilpin," Historical Society of Delaware, Papers no. 34. Wilmington, 1902. 17 pp.

Lunt, Dudley C. *The Bounds of Delaware.* Wilmington, 1947. 69 pp.; also in *Delaware History* 2 (March 1947): 1–40.

————. *The Farmers Bank 1807–1957.* Philadelphia, 1957. 308 pp.

Lyle, Charles T. "The George Read II House: Notes on its History and Preservation," *The Delaware Antiques Show*, 1986, 73–79.

MacDonald, Betty Harrington. *Historic Landmarks of Delaware and the Eastern Shore.* Wilmington, 1963. 110 pp.

"Market and Town Hall: View," *Monograph Series Recording the Architecture of the American Colonies and the Early Republic,* ser. 16, no. 6 (1930): 334.

Maynard, W. Barksdale. "New Castle's Dutch Tile House of 1687: Fraud or Genuine?" *Delaware History* 29 (Spring–Summer 2001).

————. "The Road Not Taken," *Colonial Williamsburg*, Spring 2001, 36–41.

McCready, Eliza Wolcott. "The George Read (II) House," *The Delaware Antiques Show*, 1972, 43–51.

McIntire, Nicholas S. *The Best of "Behind the Times": Selected Columns about New Castle.* New Castle [New Castle Historical Society], 1986. 316 pp.

———. *William Penn and New Castle.* New Castle [William Penn Landing Commemoration Committee], 1982. 15 pp.

McIntyre, John T. *Blowing Weather.* New York, 1923. 407 pp.

Meg, Elizabeth. *Packet Alley, A Magic Story of Now and Long Ago.* New York, 1951. 182 pp. [pseud. of Elizabeth Wenning Goepp and Margaret Webb Sanders.]

Miller, Estelle K. *A Visit to Old New Castle.* Wilmington, 1970.

Monigle, Joseph. "Reconstructing a Legend: Immanuel Church, 1980–1983," *The Delaware Antiques Show*, 1983, 57–68.

Moor, M. Margaret. "Education; New Castle." *Federal Writers' Papers at the University of Delaware*, v. 15, p. 135.

———. "New Castle Newspapers." *Federal Writers' Papers at the University of Delaware*, v. 47, p. 266.

Mumford, Richard L. "New Castle Library Company: The Founding and Early History of a Subscription Library 1811–1850," *Delaware History* 11 (October, 1965): 282–300.

Munroe, John A. *Delaware Becomes a State.* Drawings by Albert Kruse. Newark, Del., 1953. 29 pp.

———. *Federalist Delaware*, 1775–1815. New Brunswick, N. J., 1954. 286 pp.

———. "Senator Nicholas Van Dyke of New Castle," *Delaware History* 4 (June 1951): 207–226.

Nash, Gary B. "Governor Francis Nicholson and the New Castle Expedition of 1696," *Delaware History* 11 (April, 1965): 229–239.

National Geographic Society. *Guide to Small Town Escapes.* Washington, D.C., 2000. 352 pp.

*Bibliography*

"New Castle...300 Years," *Delaware Cavalcade* 1 (Spring 1951): 10–13.

New Castle Board of Trade. *New Castle, Delaware.* New Castle, 1915. Unpaginated. [Chiefly photographs of the town.]

"New Castle Common: How New Castle Came to Own 1000 Acres of Land," *Delaware Magazine,* July 1919, 95, 108.

*New Castle, Delaware, A Report Concerning Its History and Future.* New Castle, 1949. 12 pp.

New Castle Historic Buildings Commission. *A Short History of the Old Court House.* New Castle, 1957. 4 pp.

*The New Castle Historical Society: Its First Fifty Years.* New Castle [by the Society], 1984. 11 pp.

New Castle Library Company. *Catalogue of the Books Belonging to the New Castle Library Company.* Wilmington, 1819. 67 pp.; Philadelphia, 1840. 113 pp.

New Castle Tercentenary Commission. *New Castle Tercentenary of Dutch Settlement,* 1651–1951. New Castle, 1951. 1 p.

*New Castle, 1651–1951; Tercentenary Celebration.* 8 pp. [Program of exercises, including: The Dutch on the Delaware, An Historical Pageant, script by Jeannette Eckman.]

"Old Buildings in New Castle; Views," *American Architect and Architecture* 148 (February 1936): 49–56.

"Old New Castle Delaware," *Colonial Homes,* September–October 1980, 82–107+.

Olmert, Michael. "Delaware's Colonial Hideaway," *Historic Preservation,* June 1985, 58–63.

Osborn, Glenn A. "Should Delaware Create a Williamsburg?" *Delaware Today,* April/May 1968, 7–11+.

Pietuszka, J. B. "Preparations and the Recapture of Fort Casimir." *Federal Writers' Papers at the University of Delaware*, v. 23, pp. 344–347.

"Pilgrimage to New Castle," *House and Garden*, February 1944, 56–59.

Platt, Frederick. "New Castle—Living with History," *Early American Life*, February 1977, 56–58.

Pote, J. F. "Ancient New Castle Streets." *Federal Writers' Papers at the University of Delaware*, v. 4, p. 375.

———. "New Castle Chronology." *Federal Writers' Papers at the University of Delaware*, v. 9, pp. 133–134.

———. "Old Inhabitants of Swanwick." *Federal Writers' Papers at the University of Delaware*, v. 4, p. 377.

———. "Plot Surveyed for Quaker Meeting House and Burying Place." *Federal Writers' Papers at the University of Delaware*, v. 41, p. 18.

———. "School Held in New Castle Court House." *Federal Writers' Papers at the University of Delaware*, v. 15, p. 154.

Pratt, Richard. *A Treasury of Early American Homes*. New York, 1949. pp. 64–67.

Price, Edward A. "Jacob Alricks and his Nephew Peter Alricks," Historical Society of Delaware Papers, no. 22. Wilmington, 1898. 60 pp.

*Proceedings of the Convention of the Delaware State Held at New-Castle on Tuesday the Twenty-Seventh of August, 1776*. Wilmington, 1927. 43 pp.

Pyle, Katherine. *Once Upon a Time in Delaware*. Drawings by Ethel Pennewill Brown. Wilmington, 1911. 164 pp.; 2d ed., New York, 1927. 162 pp.

Read, William Thompson. *Life and Correspondence of George Read*. Philadelphia, 1870. 575 pp.

# Bibliography

*Records of the Court of New Castle on Delaware, 1676–1681*. Lancaster, Pa., 1904. 543 pp.; Vol. II, 1681–1699, land and probate abstract only. Ed. by Albert Cook Myers. Meadville, Pa., 1935. 254 pp.

Reed, Henry Clay, ed. "The Early New Castle Court," *Delaware History* 4 (June 1951): 227–245.

Reed, Henry Clay and Marion B. Reed. *A Bibliography of Delaware Through 1960*. Newark, Del. [University of Delaware, Institute of Delaware History and Culture], 1966.

Reference Department, Hugh M. Morris Library, University of Delaware. *Bibliography of Delaware 1960–1974*. Newark, Del. [University of Delaware], 1976. 226 pp.

Rhodes, A. J. *Buildings, Books & Blackboards: Education in New Castle from 1657–1930*. New Castle [New Castle Historical Society], 1993. 44 pp.

Riordan, Liam. "Identity and Revolution: Everyday Life and Crisis in Three Delaware River Towns," *Pennsylvania History* 64 (1997): 56–101.

Roberts, Daniel G. "The History and Archaeology of Immanuel Episcopal Church, New Castle, Delaware," *Pennsylvania Archaeologist* 57 (1987): 1–33.

Rodney, Richard Seymour. *Colonial Finances in Delaware*. Wilmington, 1928. 68 pp.

———. "Delaware Under Governor Keith, 1717–1726," *Delaware History* 3 (March 1948): 1–25.

———. "Historic Notes Relating to New Castle, Delaware," *Geographical Club of Philadelphia, Bulletin* 17 (October 1919): 138–142.

———. *Immanuel Church, New Castle.* Richmond, Va.?, 1943. 26 pp.; also in *Historical Magazine of the Protestant Episcopal Church* 12 (December 1943): 367–392.

———. *The Colonial Leader: Col. John French, of New Castle.* Society of Colonial Wars in Pennsylvania, Publications, v. 4, no. 8 (1935). 18 pp.

———. *The Development of Education in New Castle.* New Castle, 1931. 18 pp.

———. "The Old State House or Court House at New Castle," *Delaware Highways and Byways,* September 1939, 7.

Rosenthal, Melvin J., and Jerilyn H. Rosenthal. *The Jefferson House.* New Castle, 1984.

Samworth, Ellen. "New Castle (New Amstel) Religion and Education." *Federal Writers' Papers at the University of Delaware,* v. 15, pp. 113–133.

———. "Academies Before 1776." *Federal Writers' Papers at the University of Delaware,* v. 11, pp. 90–133.

Sanders, Deborah Merck. "Historic Towns: New Castle, Delaware," *Veranda,* May–June 1999, 48–64.

Sawin, Nancy C., and Janice M. Carper. *Delaware Sketch Book: An Historical Experience.* Hockessin, Del., 1976. 88 pp.

Sherwood, Mary Lou, and Nick McIntire. *A Walk in Old New Castle.* New Castle, 1974. 16 pp.

———. *The New Castle Mouse.* [children's coloring book for the 1976 bicentennial.] Dover, Del., 1975. Unpaginated.

Shinn, Earl, illus. "The Whipping-Post and Pillory at New Castle, Delaware," *Harper's Weekly,* December 12, 1868, cover illustration.

*Bibliography*

Silliman, Charles A. *A Time to Remember, 1920–1960: Picture Story of Forty Years in the History of Northern New Castle County, Delaware.* Wilmington, 1963. 160 pp.

Sipple, Shirley. *Delaware… Through the Years.* Chicago, 1948. 202 pp.

Spier, Peter. *To Market! To Market!* Garden City, N.Y., 1967. Unpaginated.

Spotswood, John Boswell. *An Historical Sketch of the Presbyterian Church in New Castle, Delaware.* Philadelphia, 1859. 39 pp.; Wilmington, 1905. 39 pp.

Sweeney, J. "Annals of the Old Dutch House, New Castle." *Federal Writers' Papers at the University of Delaware,* v. 13, pp. 1–96, 158.

Swierenga, Robert P., and Henry Lammers. "'Odyssey of Woe': The Journey of the Immigrant Ship *April* from Amsterdam to New Castle, 1817–1818," *Pennsylvania Magazine of History and Biography* 118 (1994): 303–324.

"Text of Library Charter." [New Castle Library Company.] *Federal Writers' Papers at the University of Delaware,* v. 45, pp. 159–163.

Toro, Lucille P. "The Latrobe Survey of New Castle, 1804–1805." Master's thesis, University of Delaware, 1971.

Townsend, George Alfred. "The Big Idiot." In his *Tales of the Chesapeake.* New York, 1880. p. 171–193.

Trustees of the New Castle Common. *New Castle Common.* Wilmington, 1944. 100 pp.

Tyler, David Budlong. *The Bay and River Delaware: A Pictorial History.* Cambridge, Md., 1955. 244 pp.

U. S. Office of National Parks, Buildings and Reservations. *Historic American Buildings Survey.* n.p., n.d. 38 sheets.

Vallandigham, Edward Noble. "Dover and Newcastle." In his *Delaware and the Eastern Shore*. Philadelphia, 1922. pp. 194–207.

Vila, Bob. "Coming of Age: The George Read II House," *Bob Vila's American Home*, Spring–Summer 1997, 74–80.

Virden, Katherine. *The Crooked Eye*. Garden City, N.Y., 1930. 296 pp.

Wamsley, James B. *The Brandywine Valley: An Introduction to Its Cultural Treasures*. New York, 1992. 244 pp.

Ward, Christopher L. *A Yankee Rover*. New York, 1932.

———. *Delaware Tercentenary Almanack & Historical Repository, 1938*. Newark, Del. [Delaware Tercentenary Commission], 1937. 55 pp.

———. *The Dutch and Swedes on the Delaware, 1609–64*. Philadelphia, 1930. 393 pp.

Wertenbaker, Charles. *To My Father*. New York, 1936. 499 pp.

Weslager, Clinton Alfred. "A Historic Delaware Town That Had Three Names," *The Delaware Antiques Show*, 1971, 97–103.

———. *Dutch Explorers, Traders, and Settlers in the Delaware Valley, 1609–1664*. In collaboration with A. R. Dunlap. Philadelphia, 1961. 329 pp.

———. "Dutch Settlements on the Delaware River," *de Halve Maen* 27 (October 1962).

———. "Historic New Castle," *Delaware Cavalcade*, Summer 1950, 8–9, 22–24.

———. "New Castle, Delaware, and Its Former Names," *Names* 24 (June 1976): 101–106.

———. *New Sweden on the Delaware 1638–1655*. Wilmington, 1988. 219 pp.

_____. *Peter Alrichs: A New Castle Merchant, Indian Trader.* Radnor, Pa., 1986. 15 pp.

_____. "The City of Amsterdam's Colony on the Delaware, 1656–1664; with Unpublished Dutch Notarial Abstracts," *Delaware History* 20 (1982–83): 1–26, 73–97.

_____. *The English on the Delaware: 1610–1682.* New Brunswick, N. J., 1967. 303 pp.

_____. *The Swedes and Dutch at New Castle.* Wilmington, 1987. 240 pp.

Wildes, Harry Emerson. *The Delaware.* New York, 1940. 398 pp.

Wilson, Everett B. *Fifty Early American Towns.* South Brunswick, N. J., 1966. 353 pp.

Wilson, W. Emerson. "Special October 24 Rites to Mark Dutch Surrender at New Castle," *Delaware Today*, August/September 1964, 13–14+.

Wise, Herbert C. *An Architectural Monograph: The George Read II House at New Castle.* New York, 1925. 24 pp. [White Pine Series, No. 64.]

Wise, Herbert Clifton, and H. F. Beidleman. "Colonial Town, New Castle, Delaware." In their *Colonial Architecture For Those About to Build...* Philadelphia, 1913. pp. 116–143.

Wolcott, Daniel F. "The Restoration of the Courthouse in New Castle," *Delaware History* 7 (1957): 193–206.

Wolf, George A., comp. *Ideal New Castle in the State of Delaware, as it Appears in the Year 1899.* Wilmington, n.d. 48 pp.

Wolfe, Nancy T. "Delaware Packets and the Coming of the Railroads," *Delaware History* 14 (October 1970): 98–110.

Woods, Caroline. *Haunted Delaware.* Bryn Mawr, Pa., 2000. 73 pp.

Wootten, Bayard Morgan. *New Castle, Delaware, 1651–1939.* Photographs by Bayard Wootten, text by Anthony Higgins. Boston, 1939. 27 pp. 47 plates.

Yeadon, David. *Hidden Corners of the Mid-Atlantic States.* New York, 1977. 182 pp.

Young, Clyde W. "Amstel House." *Federal Writers' Papers at the University of Delaware,* v. 18, pp. 349–353.

Zerin, Edward. "The New Castle & Frenchtown Turnpike & Railroad Company," *Maryland Historical Magazine* 92 (1997): 55–81.

*This book was typeset
by Angela Werner
in Adobe Caslon and Emigré Mrs. Eaves
on Macintosh equipment.*